Sound Preaching for Shaky Bridges

Tools for Preaching to Build and Encourage Leaders

By

Dr. Dwight Shawrod Riddick, II

Sound Preaching for Shaky Bridges
Tools for Preaching to Build and Encourage Leaders

Copyright © 2018 by Dwight Shawrod Riddick, II. All rights reserved.

No part of this book may be reproduced in any written, electronic, recording, or photocopying without written permission of the publisher or author. The exception would be in the case of brief quotations embodied in critical articles or reviews and pages where permission is specifically granted by the publisher or author.

Published By:
Final Step Publishing LLC

PO Box 1441
Suffolk, VA 23439

For Worldwide Distribution
Printed in U.S.A.

Library of Congress Control Number: 2018905948
ISBN: 978-0-9861250-3-4

Cover Design: LinaImaging Design
Copy Editing: Iron PROOF Editing Firm
Inside Cover Design: CMI Leadership Coaching, LLC

Get More Resources at www.dsriddick.com

Praise for *Sound Preaching For Shaky Bridges*

What Preachers are Saying

"In a brilliant, relevant and provocative way, Dr. Dwight Riddick challenges practitioners and preachers to engage in the work of motivation and transformation through their proclamation of the gospel. In a work that is as timely as it is instructive, Dr. Riddick reminds readers that "Preaching is the bridge that moves people and brings transformative value to the overlooked laity of any organization." This is both the journey and adventure to which he invites us: we would be well served to join him. A must read for any preacher."

Dr. Lance D. Watson, *Senior Pastor, Saint Paul's Baptist Church, Richmond, VA and*
author of Maximize Your Edge and That Was Then, This is Now

"Dr. Dwight Riddick, II, is excited about how good preaching can develop leaders and his passion shines through these pages. Readers will be inspired to try what he teaches, in pursuit of raising up leaders from the ranks of the laity to better share the gospel."

Paul Scott Wilson, *Professor of Homiletics, Emmanuel College of Victoria University, University of Toronto*

"For the troubled waters that inundate society, flood our communities and wash over our congregations, Dr. Dwight Riddick, II, offers preaching as a means to traverse such exigencies. Riddick's bridge homiletic transcends not by going merely from here to there but by daring to move through and across life's challenges. This is a timeless resource for persons desiring to proclaim a message of transformation through agitation."

Stephanie Buckhanon Crowder, Ph.D *Vice President of Academic Affairs, Dean of Chicago Theological Seminary*

"Wise, thoughtful, mature, pastoral, practical, faithful, humble, genuine, creative, inviting – the work of Dwight Riddick, II is all of these. Then add caring, collegial, rooted in love of the gospel, and passionate about the possibilities of real preaching for a real church in a real world. Read, learn, and grow!"

W. Dow Edgerton, *Professor of Ministry, Chicago Theological Seminary*

" *Sound Preaching for Shaky Bridges* is not only thought-provoking in content but ingenious in presentation. This work reminds us of this truth through an engaging reading experience that would benefit every minister of the Gospel."

Debra J Mumford, *Frank H. Caldwell Professor of Homiletics; Director of the Money Matters for Ministry Program*

"As a resident of Hampton Roads Va., a region surrounded by water, I have a profound appreciation for the importance of bridges. In this work Dr. Riddick uses "bridges" as a powerful metaphor to communicate the utility of preaching to move believers from a place of inactivity to a place of influence. A must read for pastors with a desire to make that connection!"

Rev. Dr. Kirk T. Houston Sr.
Senior Pastor Gethsemane Church, Norfolk, VA

"Dr. Riddick never disappoints, and "Sound Preaching for Shaking Bridges" certainly delivers! With both insight and content, the narrative is laid for ('shaky bridge') preaching as an open pathway connecting you to influence, to build, and to encourage those around you in becoming leaders, especially those who have been overlooked. An interesting facet Dr. Riddick provides is to not limit yourself to the place you are in—but rather to see the possibilities all around you—in other words—make/see those bridges and walk across them with all that you are. This is a powerful read that provides a unique perspective for every leader and reader—to see where they can serve others and serve the Kingdom by simply walking across the bridge."

Kathleen Patterson, Ph.D.
Professor & Director, Doctorate of Strategic Leadership Program School of Business & Leadership
Regent University

Dedication

To my late grandparents who were the pillars of my faith… My parents kept me connected to Gertie Mae and Willie Riddick along with Mary and Leroy Brite and as a result Jesus Christ was made real to me. These were four of God's greatest gifts that served as bridges for me to Jesus.

Acknowledgements

There are so many people to thank for this contribution to the preaching community. I begin with my mother Vera Riddick, who has always had a way of preaching without calling it that. She is why I know that preaching can be presented in so many different forms and be effective. Thank you to my father, Dr. Dwight Riddick, Sr. who is not only my favorite preacher by far, but he has been an example of how preaching must evolve and stay relevant. It was his dedication to excellence that prompted me to further my studies in preaching. I could not speak about preaching without granting gratitude to my anointed wife Dr. Jennell. She introduced me to the power of practical and spirit filled preaching with the use of gestures and her insistence on the Holy Spirit covering my human insufficiencies.

I must also thank the countless number of seasonal mentors, led by Pastor Terence Thomas, who have been influential in different seasons of my life. Pastor Terence added an intentional creativity to preaching as a wordsmith that I gleaned from. To my extended family members who have illustrated diversity in preaching--Pastor Anthony Copeland, Pastor Kevin White, Pastor Wendell Waller, Dr. Kirk Houston, Pastor Steven Blunt, Pastor Kim White, Pastor James Jones, Bishop William Dawson, Pastor

Angel White, and Pastor Vernard Hinton--thank you for providing so many opportunities for me to hear and converse about the details in preaching.

I would like to say thank you to the great professors that I have been privileged to study homiletics under and engage in scholarly dialogue with such as Dr. John Kinney, Dr. Frank Thomas, Dr. Paul Scott Wilson, Dr. Nathan Dell, Dr. James Harris, Dr. Dow Edgerton, Dr. Eunjoo Mary Kim, Dr. Gennifer Brooks, Dr. Rich Kirchherr, Dr. Karen Wiseman, Dr. Debra Mumford, Dr. Jeffery Japinga, Dr. Jan Schnell Rippentrop, Dr. Joy J. Moore, Dr. Clare Nolan, Dr. John Daly, and Dr. Charles Cosgrove. This group of professors, along with the 2018 cohort of the ACTS DMin preaching program, have heavily influenced the following thoughts.

These preachers have been my "great cloud of witnesses" and I am eternally grateful for their contribution to homiletics in both the academy and sanctuary.

Table of Contents

Preface I
   Preaching is a Bridge I
   Why Use Preaching as a Bridge? IV
   Why Intentional Bridge Preaching Helps IX

Chapter 1 1
   The Bridge Keepers –Preachers as Change Agents

Chapter 2 9
   Glocal Preaching – Identify the Marginalized

Chapter 3 23
   Grace to Grow – Power in the Four Pages of a Sermon

Chapter 4 33
   Whole Even When Not Healed – Embracing Every BODY

Chapter 5 47
   Details in Your Delivery –Control Your Body Language

Chapter 6 55
   Connect the Narratives – New Sound to an Old Story

Chapter 7	67
Comfort in Change – Crossing the Bridge	
Chapter 8	73
Personal Testimonies – After the Bridge is Built	
Appendix	A
About this Book - Cover Information	A
About The Bridge Photographs	B
About The Author	D
Bibliography	F
Notes	K

SHAKY BRIDGE
CENTRAL OTAGO, NEW ZEALAND

Preface

Preaching is a Bridge

    Our world is filled with rivers and streams that are crossed regularly because of well-built bridges. These bridges connect one place to another and bring value to often overlooked bodies of water that flow consistently and powerfully beneath them. Some examples include the Brooklyn Bridge in New York that soars over the easy flowing East River while connecting Manhattan to Brooklyn; the Chesapeake Bay Bridge that bends over the cold Chesapeake Bay waters while connecting the Eastern Shore with the Western Shore in Maryland; and the Golden Gate Bridge that spans over the wide and winding Golden Gate Straight while connecting San Francisco and Marin County. These structures are not only connectors for land masses and covers for fast flowing water, but they provide an image of the goal of preaching: to transform and transport. So if the rivers that lie under those bridges represent challenges that separate laity from leadership, and the land masses represent leadership offices on one side and the doors of entry into an organization on the other, then the bridge that provides travel from one side to the next and brings value to laity is preaching. Preaching is a bridge; however, it is not necessarily as steady and secure as the aforementioned structures. Yet, it is still a bridge. With this in mind, I introduce to you "Shaky Bridge Preaching."

In Central Otago, New Zealand, near Alexander, there is another structure known as the "Shaky Bridge." It is a suspension bridge built over the Manuherikia River. Prior to its construction, the only way across the Manuherikia River was by punt boat (a small flat-bottomed boat with a square cut bow used in small rivers or shallow water), and this was considered extremely risky at high tide. Preaching can also be described as risky, and the journey from laity to leadership can be unsettling and shaky; thus, this idea illustrates preaching when it is used to transform members of the laity into leaders. Preaching is a shaky bridge that connects regular, church attending worshippers to leadership positions, potential, and opportunities that were once not an option for them.

This idea is further illustrated by Shaky Bridge's *initial* use by wagons and horses and its current use for pedestrians *only*. Just as the bridge's usage evolved over time into something of greater use to those it serves, so too should preaching. By evolving over time and adjusting to reach those being served, preaching can encourage members of the laity to cross over into leadership. While in many cases only the elite "wagon and horse" like travelers are allowed to cross into the land of leadership, Shaky Bridge Preaching becomes the catalytic force that beckons the overlooked and ostracized "pedestrian pew member" (laity) to also take steps of faith and brave the uncertain trip across a Shaky Bridge. This trip is simply deciding to embrace a new sound presented by Shaky Bridge Preaching hence, our title, *Sound Preaching for Shaky Bridges.*

After its initial opening in 1879, Shaky Bridge fell into a state of neglect and was eventually repaired by a specially formed committee. It was at this time that the bridge was narrowed to foot traffic only. In the same way this bridge was neglected, it is possible that preaching intentionally to bridge the gap between laity and leadership has also been neglected. This book seeks to provide "shaky bridge" building tools to form a similar committee of preachers that will either rebuild bridges or preach purposeful sermons that lead laity across shaky bridges into the many iterations of leadership.

When preaching happens, travel and transformation begin in the sense that they either encourage or deter movement towards the leadership doors of an organization. Did you notice the digital tablet and hardcopy bible both displaying scriptures about preaching on the cover? This image is the preacher using various mediums to convey God's word to draw those coming from one generation towards the other side. It illustrates the challenge of reaching to connect with everyone no matter what method they use to grow in their God relationship. The goal is to use preaching to move laity from spectating to participating. I believe that preaching can have that effect. Indeed, preaching will either discourage people who are in between leadership offices and/or just entering an organization, or it will transform them into valuable contributors that encourage others to also move towards leadership. A person who hears the sound of this suggested Shaky Bridge Preaching can be saved from drowning in the rough waters that have separated them from leadership. "For there is no difference between Jew and Gentile—the same Lord is Lord of all and richly blesses all who call on him, for, "Everyone who calls on the name of the Lord will be saved. How, then, can they call on the one they have not believed in? And how can they believe in the one of whom they have not heard? And how can they hear without someone preaching to them?" (Romans 10:12-14 NIV) Ultimately, preaching is the bridge that moves people and brings transformative value to the overlooked laity of any organization--be it a church, community agency, or business. Welcome to Shaky Bridge Preaching.

Why Use Preaching as a Bridge?

Preaching can be thought of as a bridge because after hearing the preached word, people should feel empowered to the point of seeking leadership roles in various areas of life. Additionally, it should help people realize that they can be used by God to accomplish greatness regardless of their social status. When this happens, people of various social classes will maximize their God given potential and purpose. As a result, the body of Christ will be made healthier, so-called "elite groups" will become more diverse, and everyone will share in the work. Shaky Bridge Preaching empowers those who have been ostracized while creating awareness for elite groups that are blind to their group's systems that facilitated this ostracization. Shaky Bridge Preaching can indeed be the catalyst for laity to transform into leaders and for leaders to be proactive about the promotion of laity.

To fully understand this proposed form of transformation, let us accept the idea of Shaky Bridge Preaching as a foundation for this claim. When speaking of preaching as a bridge, we are suggesting that it will serve the role of provoking laity to change sooner than they would if there was no intentional preaching to inspire leadership. It is true that some lay members would eventually make the jump from simply attending church, existing in their communities, and working on their jobs into leadership. However, Shaky Bridge Preaching serves as a catalyst that prompts or pushes each person to move in the direction of leadership before they would have previously considered it and it expedites the time it takes for them to fully embrace their leadership potential. Shaky Bridge Preaching, as a catalyst, suggests that there will be some definitive reaction to purposeful preaching that will inspire internal and public transformation. *Without* this catalytic preaching, a person may exist as the victim of life's circumstances. However, *with* this catalytic preaching, each person is compelled to free the leader within themselves and begin the transformation process much sooner than later.

The transformation that will be experienced must be both private and public. With Shaky Bridge Preaching, there is first an internal transformation of the heart and mind that causes the listener to reconsider themselves and their current position in church, community, or the marketplace. To be clear, church is inclusive of any ministry space, community includes civic organizations and neighborhood involvement, and the marketplace is a person's place of work or vocation. This internal assessment is then conveyed by the actual pursuit of a leadership role. Whether attained or not, we know transformation has occurred when a person *seeks to acquire* a leadership role with expectation.

This expectation encourages transformation in the church, community, and marketplace so it may be indicated in a number of ways. For instance, a person could begin a leadership tract at their local church, seek a government office in their community, or apply for a managerial position on their job. These are just a few ways that expectant transformation can be seen and measured to prove that lay members have begun to seek leadership roles. It is not, however, limited to these specific actions. There are both a myriad of tangible responses as well as internal grappling with one's previous position in life that accompany the transformation process. These responses to Shaky Bridge Preaching, then, become the litmus test for transformation.

It is important to evaluate transformation in this way because the standard for leadership can seem ambiguous. For the sake of this conversation, please also understand that leadership has multiple faces. Shaky Bridge Preaching may propel a consistent pew sitting layperson to join a ministry or begin attending Bible Study all with the intent to soon be accepted into a ministry leadership training. A person may also rearrange their schedules to attend extra worship services, training sessions, or Bible enrichment activities. Transformation may cause a person to seek leadership by applying for a higher position on their job or leadership could be that same person changing the conversation at the water cooler from the usual negative gossip to positive words. Essentially, transformation towards leadership is evident when a person becomes active in their neighborhood watch program, attends a city council meeting and speaks up, or actually applies for a government position with the goal of becoming active in the decision making that affects a community.

Transformation from laity to leadership does not require a person to become a pastor, minister, deacon or ministry chairperson, mayor, principal, CEO or supervisor. A person need only to see themselves further along than they presently are and be willing to take others on the journey or help others move from where they are to another position in life. My father, Dr. Dwight Riddick, Sr. always says, "Leaders assist others in moving to a location that they would not journey to on their own or one that they did not know was an option for themselves." As previously stated, this leadership journey will be in places other than the church. For this reason, change and leadership will take on many forms and will be experienced at many levels including, but not limited to, our local church assemblies.

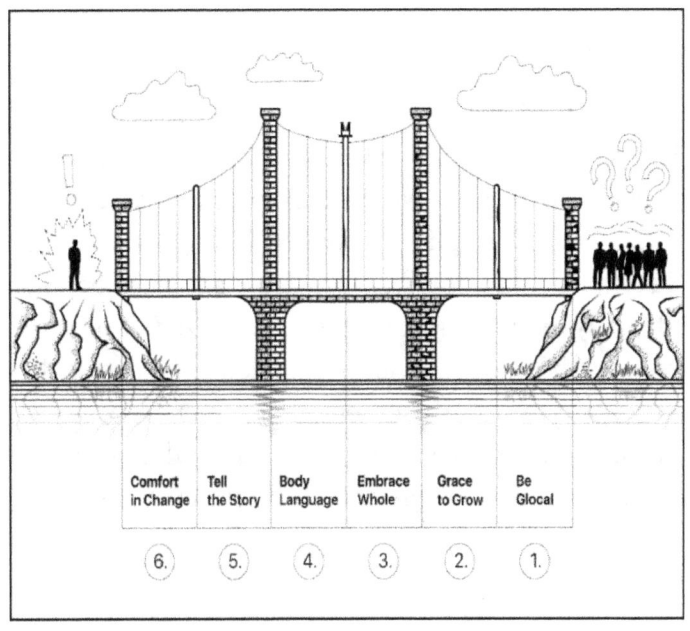

Preaching As A Bridge

Why Intentional Bridge Preaching Helps

While serving as the youth pastor of a large inner city church in Newport News, VA and now as the senior pastor of a rural congregation in Franklin, VA, I have seen a gaping distance between those who have been allowed to serve in leadership and those who are not given that same opportunity. I've wanted to believe that it is accidental, but I've come to see that it may have been intentional--not intentional because the current leaders were mean and power driven; but, instead, it was intentional because everyone was okay with the same leaders doing everything and there was no plan to change it. Most of the time leaders would just quote the 80/20 Pareto rule that says 20% of the people would typically do 80% of the work. While that may often be the case in many places, I could not readily receive that as acceptable. As I surveyed scripture, I noticed that the trend at our church was not foreign to what had been popular biblically where some were ostracized from the majority because of various ailments. The disabled were banned from the temple, women were often unnamed, and kings were made of children simply because of their pedigree when others may have been more qualified.

All of these examples, and many more, were prevalent in the Bible. This is often true today as many have been limited because of their physical disabilities, others because of past mistakes they have made, and still a larger group simply because they were not born into families that had previously held leadership roles in the church. This is where Shaky Bridge Preaching can be of great benefit because it expands the border and allows the church to become more inclusive of those it has overlooked. The Bible took this same turn when Jesus came as a bridge between the Old Testament separation and the New Testament inclusion. What you are about to experience on the following pages are a few specific examples that show how Shaky Bridge Preaching can "shake things up" a little and welcome more people into leadership.

CHARLES BRIDGE
PRAGUE, CZECH REPUBLIC

PONT JACQUES CHABAN LIFT BRIDGE
BORDEAUX, FRANCE

Chapter 1

The Bridge Keepers – Preachers as Change Agents

Let's begin our journey to provide solutions for transforming laity into leaders. Imagine standing on the shore peering across a roughly flowing river. The waters are too rough to sail or swim across. Flying over the water-filled chasm is not an option. If you attempt either of these routes, going low or flying, you will discover that both of those options would lead to failure. Assuming this is true, to get across you would have to change your mind about ways to crossover. This type of mind change is what will allow you to build a bridge while travelling through the pages of this reading. That is how you overcome this challenge. Build a bridge. Bridge building may not be the norm in our preaching, but assuming that our normal methods of sermon swimming, scripture sailing, or flying with the same ole preaching propelled aircrafts have not led people into the leadership roles that are available, I would say it may be time to address change and try bridge building. When I say address, I mean that change must be provided in illustration before it is expected to be seen in application. People will not change until the preaching and preacher are willing to change. Who else is better suited and qualified to show the change we are expecting to see in others than the preacher who is initiating the change? Who else could lead people successfully across the bridge towards leadership than the bridge keeper? The bridge keeper's job is to lower and raise the bridge so as to allow or disallow constant traffic flow. In the same way, it is first the preacher who will allow or disallow laity's transformation into leadership. Just as a bridge keeper indicates when we are to advance or be still, the preacher shows laity whether they can advance or be still. All of this happens by simply observing if the preacher is preaching a message of change with or without changing their methods. If change is going to take place in the pew, it must be seen in the pulpit. It may be evident in other areas outside of the pulpit as well; however, for the purposes of this journey, change must take place *with the preaching* in order for change to take place *in the hearts* of the laity. The need for change is not new, but it is necessary. The following excerpt helps us understand this more clearly:

> "Though the church still tolerates a man behind the pulpit, she has become quite concerned as to what he says, how he says it, and how much of her time he takes to say it! It hasn't always been this way. A retooling of the

modern church service has been hammered out in America's seminaries over the past few decades. Up-and-coming churchmen – many with a God given passion and untapped gift to preach – are taught to keep their Bible lecture (if retained as part of the Sunday Service) positive, palatable, trendy, and above all short." [1]

There must be some indicators that show change in the preacher and in the preaching content. As new leaders arise and current leaders are invited to either change their role or share their work load, all parties will need to understand how to embrace change. This happens by the preacher becoming an example of change, by his/her detail in the delivery, and by showing said change with varied styles of storytelling. In doing so, change won't affect value and it will create a new level of comfort for transition.

While the need for embracing change may be a concept mentioned in detail later in this reading, it is really the core of our entire conversation and, thus, deserves attention now.

> ...show change in the preacher and in the preaching content.

Change must take place. As you go forward, I ask that you read with a mind that is open and receptive to adding these tools to your preaching style arsenal. Remember, change is not bad; change is just different. Honestly, it is why in the previous paragraphs I have

> Remember, change is not bad; change is just different.

intentionally used the word "change" so often. I would like you to get use to hearing and embracing change for it is what makes the bridge so "shaky." Dr. Lance Watson once preached a sermon about change at the nationally renowned *Hampton University Ministers' Conference* that I vividly remember to this day. It has become one of my personal all time favorite sermons ever preached. It was entitled, "That Was Then, This is Now." His message illuminated the transition in leadership between Moses and Joshua. He began with an extended run on all the things that Moses had meant to the Israelites. He noted that Moses had been an "intercessor, deliver, manna distributor, quail dispenser, and water supply boy" in addition to his other responsibilities. Dr. Watson then said that "our longing for what was inhibits our ability of what is and even what can be." He then proclaimed that although Moses *had been* important, he was yesterday's news because, now,[2] "Moses is dead!" The climax for me in this message is when he then stated, "that was then and this now."

Later, I was elated to find that he provided this same idea in a book with the same title. He begins chapter seven of that book by saying,

> *"If you live long enough, you will go through some changes. Life is full of changes. Some we can anticipate, others catch us completely off*

guard. Every life is loaded with landmarks, marked by milestones, and pierced with turning points."[2]

It is this statement that urges us be a part of the change instead of waiting for it to catch us off guard. All of the upcoming forms of preaching are designed to help facilitate an anticipated change. Change is not bad, change promotes the transition of laity into leadership. This type of transition is not outside of what is expected of us as preachers. We are change agents. Even when it seems difficult, we cannot give up on instigating positive change. To neglect change is to forfeit the power of God that we preach about. Neglecting change is to forget about God. "God is present in every situation and every complication. While we are struggling to deal with changes in our bodies, lives, relationships, businesses, careers, and health, remember God is there – search for God." [3]We, too, must search for God in our preaching and believe that when He is found, transition will take place. What we do not want to do is linger too long in the same place.

My father, Dr. Dwight Riddick Sr., writes about a moment when the children of Israel were challenged to cross over the river in Deuteronomy 2:13 but kept circling the mountain instead. "'Now then, proceed to cross over the Wadi Zered.' So we crossed over the Wadi Zered."(Deuteronomy 2:13) In his book, *Does Preaching Have A Future,* he comments on this scripture saying,

"It was necessary for the Israelites to cross the brook if they were to experience God's best. They had not been delivered from Egypt just to remain in the same place. The blessing that God had in store for them was still ahead. The brook they had to cross represented a barrier that kept them from the destiny God had in store for them. Perhaps one of the reasons they circled the mountain so many times was because of that brook. Could they have seen the brook as a challenge or an obstacle they had to overcome? Rather than take on the challenge or seize the opportunity, they remained in the place of familiarity."[4]

Let us learn from their mistake. Let us not become bridge keepers that keep God's children from crossing over into God's best. Let's be willing to make the change and open the doors to greater with this bridge. When change occurs, we begin Shaky Bridge Preaching.

> When change occurs, we begin what I call 'Shaky Bridge Preaching'.

Shaky Bridge Preaching may not be easy, nor will it always be immediately accepted. It will bring feelings of joy *and* danger. This is what Dr. Frank Thomas calls a "terrible joy of dangerous preaching." He notes that, "… preaching is also terrible and dangerous. It is terrible because, if we do our job well, preaching troubles and shakes the foundations of this world."[5] This is why I call it Shaky Bridge Preaching.

BROOKLYN BRIDGE
NEW YORK CITY, NEW YORK

BRIDGE OF THE AMERICAS
BALBOA, PANAMA

Chapter 2

Glocal Preaching – Identify the Marginalized

Many congregants have embraced the notion that they are not equal to other members who may be in leadership. They have not just been marginalized, but they have become comfortable living as unrecognized outsiders. These outsiders are what Eunjoo Mary Kim refers to as the "other" in her book *Preaching in an Age of Globalization*. In order to help the "other" know they are valuable, our preaching should highlight groups that are further beyond the margins than we are. Preaching that informs a congregation with what takes place in other countries presses the boundaries beyond the locally marginalized "others." The awareness that there are "others" who need help will empower those who traditionally only look for leaders to help them. This is the idea behind "glocal preaching." When people hear about the amount of poverty in Haiti, lack of drinking water as a basic need in Cambodia, mudslides that murder kids in Sierra Leone, or other natural disasters on the outside of the United States, it

> Our preaching is more than a message about God. It is a message about God and humanity.

allows them to view their personal experiences from a larger perspective. In most cases, the problems that once were used to keep them from leadership no longer disqualify them when compared to these other global catastrophes. It is preaching that sits global issues into the lap of the local attendee. Glocal preaching can empower a person to abandon the victim mentality and help them see themselves as privileged. However, glocal preaching cannot be achieved until the preacher has properly identified the culture of their church. This is done by asking questions like, "How do the listeners listen?" or "What are they hearing when I use certain words?" Once the culture has been uncovered, glocal preaching can begin.

Glocal preaching is a combination of reaching those that are local and addressing what takes places globally. It is preaching made to be a key component of reaching the marginalized. Laura Tisdale suggests that the Gospel must go through and then beyond. It should not be limited to our own culture. It must feed the majority and the minority groups of our church. Our preaching must help everyone expand their perspective of God. When this happens, we increase our ability to touch more people in our preaching. The more people we touch, the greater the chance that we are able to develop new leaders. Our preaching is more than a message about God. It is a message about God and humanity. Humanization Theology, which is the discernment of what God is doing in our globalized world in order to make and keep human life, sheds more insight on this. The idea of Humanization Theology is that God's humanization activity is a communal process towards the liberation of God's creation on earth. Our preaching must reflect that truth. Our preaching must speak to how God interacts with humans--all humans--with no more attention to one person than another. This is expressed in Acts 10 after Cornelius, a regular man, had a Godly vision and then sent additional, regular men to connect with a regular man named Peter who had his own flaws.

All of these ordinary men gathered and from this synergy Peter says, "…Of a truth I perceive that God is no respecter of persons: But in every nation he that feareth him, and worketh righteousness, is accepted with him." (Acts 10:34,35 KJV) These two verses not only introduce the idea of local acceptance; but, with men traveling to find Peter, they speak to global assimilation. When the distance between these men is highlighted, it helps local congregations see themselves as not only valuable to those around them but, also, to those who live beyond their borders. In the same way men were sent to Peter, people need to hear that they are being sent to find Peter-like individuals. Then, in the same way Peter ministered we can empower our listeners to serve. Peter apparently had a ministry in the place he was in but he also ministered to those who resided outside of his current location. This is an example of glocal ministry at work and this is a ministry that should be preached.

Additionally, it is possible to have a missing segment of people that is sitting in the pews every week simply because their perspective of life has not been considered. In order to find this missing group, we must preach about those who are often overlooked in scripture. John McClure speaks of the deconstruction of what we know and think. McClure argues that we should "erase" the preconceived ideas that we take into a text and culture.

> ...to find this missing group, we must preach about those who are often overlooked in scripture.

We cannot assume that our way as preachers is always right nor should we assume that the current leadership has all of the answers. We must strive in our preaching to find the "other" perspective. This happens when a sermon is preached sympathetically, empathetically, and/or interpathetically.

Sympathetic preaching says, "I understand because I have a similar experience." Empathetic preaching says, "I understand although I have had no similar experience." And interpathetic preaching says, "I cannot understand your experience but I will strip myself of my own ideas to stand in your place." Standing in the place of another is how we connect locally. This local look at our congregation keeps us mindful of the groups that are often marginalized through preaching. Dr. Stephanie Crowder recounts an experience where she was challenged to write about the Bible's perspective of motherhood. She chose this topic because it seemed that there was an entire group that had been neglected in her writing. So, after considering what she calls a "hole" in her scholarship, her solution to missing these groups was to "make it plain." I believe that what she self-proclaimed to miss in her writing is similar to the many groups we, too, miss in our preaching. I agree with Crowder when she says,

> *"I need to combine my way of thinking about the Bible and how I get meaning from it with my social identity as a mother, professor, wife, scholar, and preacher. I could no longer speak, get my check, and leave. Mothers longed for me to use my gifts in the academy and the church to help 'make it plain,' 'make motherhood plain.' Women had to have more."*
> 6

The idea of "more" that Crowder speaks of is preaching that will "make it plain" and go beyond motherhood to reach the margins. When people require more of us, it begs for us to search for all who feel as if the Bible and preaching have somehow overlooked them. Crowder focuses on mothers and presents the bible from a womanist perspective by highlighting stories that are often not preached or mentioned such as those about women like Hagar, Rizpah, Bathsheba, and Zebedee's wife.

The story of the Canaanite women is another great example. Crowder uses this account to reach mothers who are on the margin by helping to redefine the roles of mothers who work out of home as well as those who work from home. It is important to note that it is not a matter of whether or not you are a mother because you work out of the house but, instead, "Perhaps the crux of the matter is redefining the definition of work to include both mothers whose nine-to-five is at their residence and those who punch a clock at work."[7] This highlights the necessity of redefining common terms in order to be more inclusive of historically marginalized groups. We can often get so comfortable with church conversation and Christian lingo that we miss groups altogether. "Jesus did not speak in spiritual terms or use religious jargon. He spoke to the relevant need of the woman. By no means was this a

> We can often get so comfortable with church conversation and Christian lingo that we miss groups altogether.

watering down of the gospel. Rather, he was seeking to build a bridge whereby he could get the woman's attention."[8] The replacing of too much religious talk with redefined terms allows a reconnection with groups who were once marginalized. These groups include women, addicts, the handicapped, those who have been incarcerated, the diseased, senior citizens, children, and so many others who may simply be different than the majority or different from the preacher. This is why being sympathetic, empathetic, and interpathetic are so essential to Shaky Bridge Preaching.

On one occasion, I attempted to incorporate all of these concepts while "bridge preaching" Luke 15:7-32. This is the story of a prodigal son, a loving father, and a seemingly jealous brother. I have typically heard and preached it from the perspective of the sons and also the father. However, with glocal preaching in mind, and a goal of reaching those who are marginalized, I sought to find the "other" in the text that is often overlooked. I wanted to thoroughly engage this text with transcontextual hermeneutics. It is Eunjoo Mary Kim

> The preacher who reads the text both within and beyond her [his] local congregation is challenged to read it by way of thinking through others.

who describes this hermeneutic style as, "The preacher who reads the text both within and beyond her [his] local congregation is challenged to read it by way of thinking through others."[9]

It was this challenge of being transcontextual, presenting the sermon for a local congregation while allowing them to hear about a much larger but often discredited group, that I faced when searching through this text. To start this process I recruited a small team of random members from our church to assist in gaining a variety of perspectives. This team approach to sermon preparation was one of many ways that I thought to be transcontextual. It worked. The team had so many great insights that I would have never thought of simply because we all have different life experiences. One member began to speak of her struggle as a parent to please both of her children without being accused of doing too much for one while neglecting the other. She was connecting with the father in the prodigal son story in a way that I had never imagined. She highlighted how overlooked he often is because it is rare for anyone to consider how painful it is to be accused of treating one child better than another when in fact that is not the parent's intent. The group immediately joined in the conversation and we agreed that this issue was present in the life of the father in Luke 17 and in the lives of many in our congregation. However, I was not fully convinced that he was the only "other."

While this was a very unique perspective of the text and our life problems, I felt a tug to keep searching. By virtue of the fact that so many members of the group could relate, I felt as if this person was too common. After a deeper look and what I believe to be a revelation from God, I noticed that there was mention of a "servant" threaded throughout the message. The servant or servants have no name(s), get no recognition, and are rarely spoken of, but they do all of the work. This was a way to identify the "other." This servant represented the many hard working, never recognized members of our congregation that have not been given a chance. The servants were with the father, the lost son, and the son that was at home. The servants were in the same scenarios as all three main characters. The servants were also the ones that provided solutions to their pains, problems, and pinching. Yet, the servants did not always fully feel the agony of each. The servants were there hiding in plain sight. Or maybe, they were not hiding, they were just present and invisible. The servant experiences what Sang Hyun refers to as "a liminal space or an in between space, a social limbo created by a person's leaving his or her social structure, and not yet having returned to that structure or to a new one."[10] The servant was not on the same level with them, but he did not have his own place either.

I exposed during the closing of the sermon that I was actually preaching the sermon from the first person perspective as the servant. I attempted to show that the listening congregation did not notice who I was because the servant is often the "other" that is overlooked. The servant does a lot of work behind the scenes so I reimaged the servant from just some unknown character of the story and presented him as the party planner. I must be honest, this approach to the text felt like what McClure calls "Exiting the House of Tradition."[11] This is simply a suggestion that in preaching we all must do something that is uncomfortable in order to arrive at a different conclusion than normal. It was different for me; however, it was leaving what was comfortable in hermeneutical norms, and identifying this character during the preaching moment, that made it an effective way to transform laity.

> ... glocal preaching reaches the marginalized.

The use of this transcontextual vantage point, while simultaneously connecting the prodigal son's location in a foreign land to globally oppressed employees, helps illustrate how glocal preaching reaches the marginalized. Simply naming foreign countries and their living conditions helps your local listener expand their perspective on what a hardship is. In one sermon, laity expressed sympathy for another country, empathized with an oppressed employee eating pig slop in another country, and interpathetically connected with a servant that had been overlooked.

This illustration is only one of many examples of how glocal preaching helps bridge the gap between laity and leadership. Depending on the make up of the congregation, this could be considered a risky message. Moreover, it could also be considered what Dr. Frank Thomas calls a "Dangerous Sermon." Thomas says, "Dangerous preaching challenges our established notions about religion and its place in society."[12] Because it has often been religion that has placed so many people outside the boundaries of blessings that we preach about, we must build a bridge to facilitate reconnection.

This bridge is built when glocal preaching is a priority for the preacher who cares enough to imitate David Augsburger who says,

> *"Bracketing my own beliefs, I believe what the other believes, see as the other sees, value what the other values, and feel the consequent feelings as the other feels them."*[13]

This is the goal of glocal preaching. It is simply to become one with the "other." It is mentally sitting beside them and getting to know each person for who he/she is. Glocal

> **When the preacher cares enough for everyone and not just an elite few, glocal preaching has an opportunity to transform laity into leaders.**

preaching requires us to care. When the preacher cares enough for everyone and not just an elite few, glocal preaching has an opportunity to transform laity into leaders. Leaders that are made through glocal preaching have a higher respect for those who are marginalized because they, too, have been in that overlooked position. Furthermore, current leaders, who encourage promotion because of their own glocal perspective, become much more compassionate towards those who are in the "other" groups.

Overall, Shaky Bridge Preaching provides an opportunity for everyone to connect in their current place and then begin the journey towards shared leadership in their own way.

MONO VALE GARDEN BRIDGE
CHRISTCHURCH, NEW ZEALAND

GOLDEN GATE BRIDGE
SAN FRANCISCO, CA

CHAPTER 3

GRACE TO GROW – POWER IN THE FOUR PAGES OF A SERMON

The next aspect of Bridge Preaching deals with identifying the sermon structure that provides the best delivery of transformative content. How can we build a sermon that inspires people to want leadership for themselves? Preaching with a "Four Pages of a Sermon" format does more than provide a preaching structure; it also introduces the grace of God. One of the many barriers for a person to believe in themselves as a potential leader is the idea that they are not worthy of a leadership position. This feeling of unworthiness creates a disconnect from laity to leadership. It creates a disconnect from the church at large. This is not a new challenge for laity. Paul Wilson argues that this disconnect happens because grace is often absent from our preaching today. It is not always done on purpose or consciously. But, more times than not, the lack of grace or good news in a sermon is because of how we structure the sermon from the beginning. Frank Thomas speaks of structural defects in the sermonic system that increase anxiety in listeners and among them is the missing Gospel. "The preacher is an expert at analyzing the problem (the bad news) but a novice at concrete Gospel solutions that give people hope, and therefore the sermon has more bad news than good news."[14] Can you imagine how difficult it must be to envision yourself moving up the ranks into leadership when all you have heard is bad news, criticism, and judgment? The heavy doses of bad news that may often be heaved from our pulpits can cause a person to feel disconnected.

The feeling of unworthiness blankets any aspirations of leadership because it presents a space in fellowship and, seemingly, in one's relationship with God and those around them. Barbara Lundblad notes that, "We're not the first generation to sense deep estrangement-separation from ourselves, from one another and from something or someone beyond ourselves."[15] If we fail to sense this separation created in bad news preaching, we may not acknowledge the need to build a bridge that reconnects people to themselves and to each other. Not recognizing the separation is an internal structure malfunction of our preaching that must be addressed in the preaching preparation and then reinforced in order to build a true leader. If we do not deal with separation, laity will attempt to work and serve their way back together when, in actuality, there is never an appropriate amount of work, service, or action that can completely qualify a person for servant leadership. True leaders must depend on God's unmerited favor known as grace. When grace is preached in place of the need for a person to perform in order to be accepted, we begin to qualify everyone for leadership. Laity needs to hear more grace preaching and less about performance in order for transformation to take place. By performance I mean preaching that asserts laity must act a certain way and complete a particular task in order for God to bless, heal, protect, or care for them. This is common in dialectic styled preaching that often presents a "three step must do this, in order to get that" type of preaching style. This style in and of itself is not wrong; however, too much "must do this" preaching dilutes grace which says despite our wrong doing, lack of doing, and above all of our correct doing, God desires to qualify each person for a blessing. In place of personal performance there is transformative power in the grace of God alone. Performance preaching insists that people have to follow the choreography God has assigned in order to be accepted. This should not be the case. "Someone has asked us to dance, and we don't have to worry about knowing the steps. This is grace to the ungraceful."[16] Godly grace is presented in two forms. It is presented in knowing the person doing the preaching and in the amount of grace included in the content of preaching.

> **True leaders must depend on God's unmerited favor known as grace.**

Let's first examine the preacher. I have learned that one of the most underrated aspects of preaching is our body language. This is problematic to preaching because, according to Albert Mehrabian, communication is 55% body language, 38% voice, and only 7% words. If we place all of our emphasis on the words we use, we miss a vast portion of what laity receive in communication. Everything we do communicates, so why not be intentional about it? Another reason to be intentional about body language during the preaching moment can be found in the deficit vs. sufficient model. This model suggests that having a deficit is when you lack something so you need it, versus sufficiency that says you have everything already but must know how to use it.

In the preaching moment, we must recognize when we lack the proper communication tools versus when we actually do have the communication in our body language and just have not properly used our body language to complement and help convey the message. Proper use of body language increases the chance of proper communication. In either case, we must examine not just what we say but how we say it to evaluate whether there are aspects of our delivery that we should develop or aspects of our preaching that we must enhance to help with the reception of grace. We do not want to use words that say "you are accepted" but then convey them in a tone or manner that suggests otherwise. The goal isn't just for a person to hear the message, but they must also receive it. It is the message of grace that says,

> "You are accepted. You are accepted by that which is greater than you, and the name of which you do not know. Do not ask for the name now; perhaps you will find it later...Simply accept the fact that you are accepted!"[17]

Professor Claire Nolan mentions that our body is triggered by feelings. For example, your body adjusts to anger by making you run, increasing your heart rate, pumping adrenaline, and causing a shortness of breath. This is only important because how you feel when you are preaching will often be felt by the congregation. Even the sound of our voice is based on how we feel because the voice box is unprotected and exposed. It is for this reason that a preacher must have some self-awareness before and while attempting to deliver messages about developing leaders. A person's ability to receive the message of grace may be contingent upon the preacher's clarity, invitation, and authenticity. These three essentials are not found in content but in voice inflection and body language. Clarity is the ability to properly articulate

> **Clarity is the ability to properly articulate intellectually, emotionally, or spiritually.**

intellectually, emotionally, or spiritually. The invitation is found when voice quality and body language beckon hearers to listen and be involved. Finally, authenticity deals with the sense that what is being said is true and embedded in the speaker's beliefs or life experiences. What connects this to grace is the immediate presentation of an imperfect person attempting to convey a message of grace to similarly imperfect people. So, on one hand, preachers should be mindful of their voice and body language; but, at the same time, this is a constant reminder that whenever we stand as preachers we are allowed to do so only because of God's grace. We will discuss the importance of overall body language later, but for now I hope this helps explain how body language and grace connect.

After putting every exercise into practice that physically makes this moment of preaching possible, we must remember that the preaching moment itself is a moment where God is bestowing grace upon the preacher. Have you noticed that church, communities, and workplaces are no longer homogenous? None of those places have one type of person or personality. All of these environments have many different people existing in them at the same time. Our congregations are diverse as well and require a true connection that begins with standing to preach and continues with delivering a message that keeps everyone on the same level. A few very practical methods in showing grace through preaching is managing body language and voice inflection. Henry Mitchell, the creator of the "Preaching as Celebration" style, explains that your emotions can either attract or run listeners away. Mitchell presses for the need of emotive preaching. The emotions can be shared by all, thus creating a synergy that places the pulpit and pew, the preacher and laity, and emerging leaders and existing leaders in the same emotional place. He argues that preaching should include some true backstory that connects people to the preacher's real life experiences.

The backstory of the preacher is an illustration of God's grace that creates an inclusive environment. And a grace filled environment is essential to transformation. The "Celebration Preaching" style, also presented by Dr. Frank Thomas, introduces four movements in place of four pages. These movements are to explain a text by sharing the textual situation, complication, resolution, and celebration. This storytelling format, which we will be detailed later in the reading, is less instructive and, as a result, also less destructive. The shared moment of storytelling in either "Preaching as Celebration" or the "Four Pages of a Sermon" style allows others to feel as if they are connected to the preacher. This connection through sermon style becomes an invisible illustration of grace that may be unseen but can definitely be felt. These are two styles available for productive Shaky Bridge Preaching.

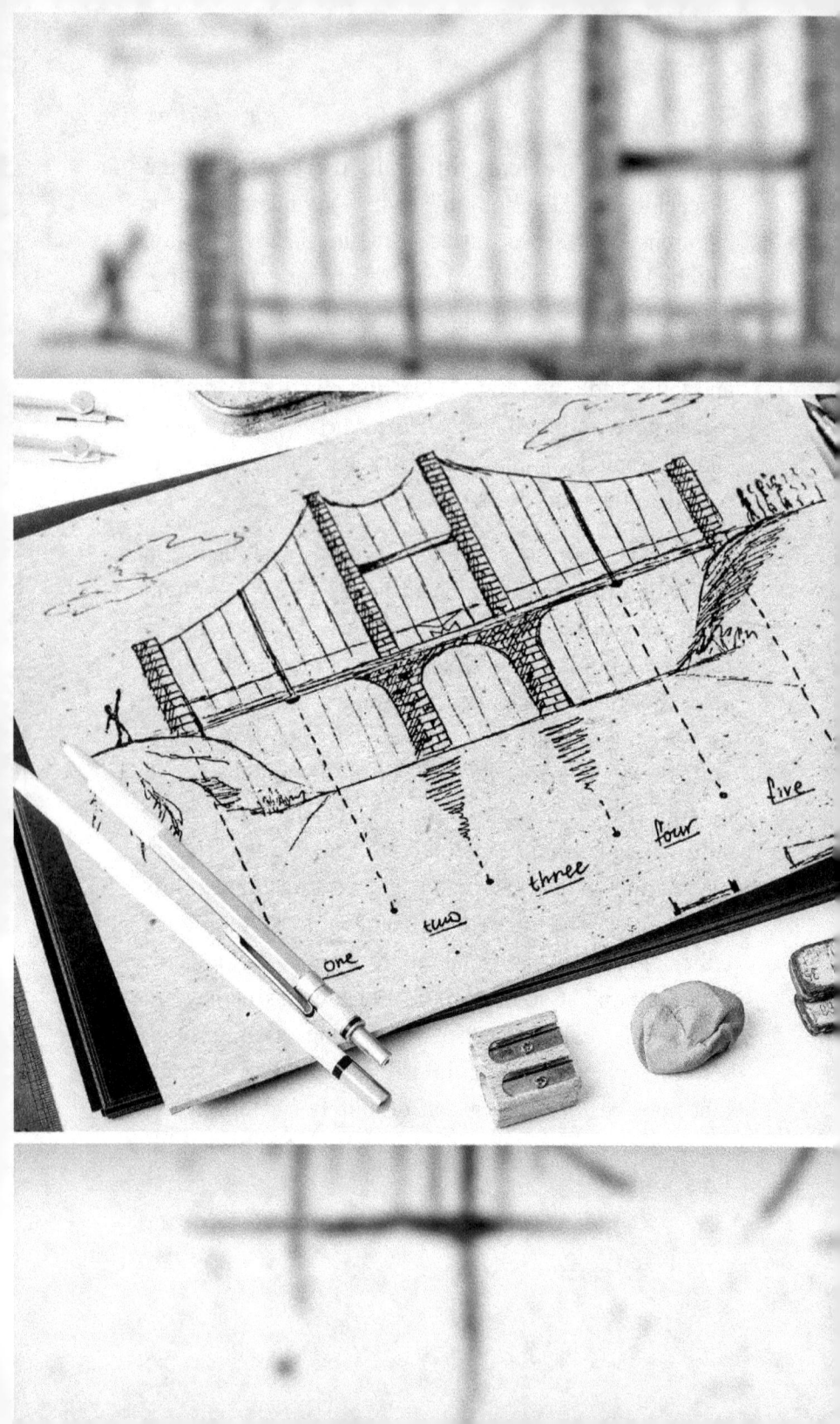

HUSSAINI HANGING BRIDGE
HUNZA, PAKISTAN

KOTMALE OYA
HORTON PLAINS, SRI LANKA

Chapter 4

Whole Even When Not Healed – Embracing Every Body

Once grace has been fairly dispersed and the preacher as the delivering tool is examined, there is a moment in bridge building that laity must also be examined. When identifying that God's grace qualifies all laity, we must then *reach towards* all laity. The emphasis here is on all people being considered true contenders for leadership. There are some groups with which the church in general has neglected to connect. More personally, I know our church has been negligent in seeking leadership potential from those who appeared physically disabled, impaired, or handicapped. There was no spoken rule, it was just a commonly accepted occurence. The church has often operated under the unspoken idea that a person who is somehow physically disabled is also disallowed a place in leadership. There has also been a misguided perception of those who are able-bodied (i.e. appear physically healthy) as being of high social standing and those who are not as somehow falling into less respected, marginalized groups. We see it often when women, children, and the elderly are placed in the same category but in a very different category than seemingly healthy men. There is an unstated prejudice towards one group while the other is often overlooked. Even if someone becomes ill during their leadership tenure, they may remain in position but are often stripped of responsibility. It is almost as if the assumed physical weakness of this group disqualifies them from leadership. There is a social norm that places those who are not able-bodied in a group that *needs help* instead of realizing that they can *be helpful*. When this social construct is in place, it automatically eliminates those who are not able-bodied from consideration for leadership.

While this construct is not blatantly in place, it is quite a rarity to see pastors in wheelchairs, leaders who are hearing impaired, or worship leaders who are crippled. Many in these physical conditions have been reduced in social status simply because of their physical inabilities. There should be preaching that promotes those physically limited to apply their faith, serve, and perform in leadership with their skillset. While their performance may not be the same as those who are able-bodied, it is of no lesser value. It may appear limiting to your organization to discuss enabling someone who is disabled, but this is just a shaky bridge not a broken one; so, we must bridge the gap. Naturally, physical inabilities create an uneasiness for leaders who are already serving. However, what we often fail to realize is that most seemingly healthy leaders are only "temporarily-able bodied" as Debra Mumford puts it. One life situation could land any of us in the place of physical limitation. We would easily attempt to apply our skill and overlook our disability, and there should be preaching that does the same for all. People do not have to be disconnected because of physical disability. They are separated but should be connected. We must using Shaky Bridge Preaching to create this connection.

> One life situation could land any of us in the place of physical limitation.

And, so, this preaching should speak about God reigning and accepting physically disabled persons as whole. In so doing, we allow the inclusion of many more potential leaders. Additionally, this type of preaching empowers the socially handicapped and, thus, transformation takes place in two forms. First, the content in preaching causes those who are disabled to feel as if they belong and are a valued part of the congregation. Secondly, the awareness of the disabled in our congregations helps those in leadership see that they have unknowingly oppressed and omitted an entire segment of the congregation from leadership.

Dr. Kathleen Patterson, Director of the School of Strategic Leadership at Regent University led a lecture on "The Advantage of the Last Zero." This lecture emphasized the importance of those we treat like the number zero. She noted that most people mistreat and devalue the number zero. She then proceeded to show a list of prime numbers. Dr. Patterson suggested that because these numbers were prime, they were given priority treatment and were made the primary source of all we do. She then proceeded to place a zero behind each number. Instantly the number two (2) became twenty (20), the number twenty (20) became two hundred (200), and three (3) became thirty (30). Do you see how valuable what we consider to be a zero (0) can be? Her point was clear--anything or anyone that has a zero added to it increases its value. We too often treat the disabled as zeros all the while misunderstanding their value.

This is not just a current challenge; it has existed since the days of antiquity. If a person had leprosy, they were pressed to the margins. A woman who had experienced internal bleeding was relegated to the outskirts of the city. There was even a young man who was dismissed and given absolutely no consideration for leadership because he was blind. The question was asked, "Who sinned, this man or his parents that he would be born blind?" as if to somehow attribute his physical illness to a mistake that had been made in order to disallow him from following Jesus. Our perspective of the impaired,

Whole Even When Not Healed

disabled, and handicapped must be reexamined and adjusted in order to properly build a bridge and start transformation.

The biblical account of Mephibosheth and Ziba provides insights into a method by which we could start to build this bridge. I preached a single sermon from 2 Samuel 9:1-12 (David and Mephibosheth) entitled, "You Have A Seat At The Table."

The major message of this sermon presented the conflict of Ziba having to somehow help an overlooked Mephibosheth maximize his invitation from King David to dine at the king's table. The introduction literally provided a picture of people that had dealt with the feeling of loneliness or of being neglected while in the presence of many. It also highlighted a real life story of Tricha Zorn, a blind swimmer who has yet to be celebrated like Michael Phelps despite achieving a similar world champion and gold medal-winning feat. Michael Phelps is a great swimmer and received commercials and endorsements for his accomplishments, but Tricha Zorn—a blind swimmer—won gold medals and no one knows her name. The goal was to intentionally connect to the physically disabled segment of worshippers and show

> This style or focus in preaching of not neglecting the disabled also brings awareness to those who are physically healthy.

them a portrait of themselves in scripture where God both used and blessed someone who was in a similar situation.

This goal was based in part on a portion of Jana Childers' book, *Performing the Word, Preaching as Theater,* where it states, "It was Martin Luther who developed the notion of preaching as an 'encounter', a notion re-appropriated and popularized by twentieth-century neo-orthodoxy."[18] When listeners experience scripture from a vantage point where they are able to see themselves in the text, the encounter increases the potential for transformation. This style or focus in preaching of not neglecting the disabled also brings an awareness to those who are physically healthy. Another goal was to get each "temporarily able bodied" person to know that we, like Ziba, are to help all neglected people get all that God has for and from them just as Mephibosheth did.

According to Debra Mumford, Nancy Eisland argues that, "people with disabilities of all types form a minority group because they are excluded and persecuted by the majority of people who are temporarily able bodied."[19] We are all either disabled or "temporarily able bodied," so either way this message applies and is profitable. The idea of this message is that there is a shared responsibility for the disabled. Mephibosheth was hurt because someone else dropped him and this is a real life scenario for many who have become impaired or disabled because of no fault of their own. He was not crippled because of any misconduct or sin that he committed; but, instead, he had been the victim of a disabling incident that was totally beyond his control. Noting this during the preaching moment can turn the message from a "him and them" mindset to a "we and us" connection. The goal is to shift from attributing disabilities to a person's fault to making it everyone's responsibility to care for the victim.

According to Charles Bartow, this is important. He mentions,

> *"The 'us' referred to in the kerygmatic expectation we bring to the public reading and hearing of Scripture is not just a collection of individuals having no common identity. It is instead, that body or ecclesial community chosen by God – and by God alone – to bear witness to the divine presence in the midst of the world through the word and sacrament."*[20]

When the disabled in "the room" of our churches become an 'us' issue, our congregations become much more understanding and accepting of a broader group. During the preaching moment, I found that there was a connection between this point in the message and the listeners based on the constant head nodding and occasional "amens" being shouted aloud. While there were many other practical points in the sermon, the main ideas were that we should enjoy God's grace and we all are qualified for leadership. The entire sermon closed with a dual empowerment

> The goal is to shift from attributing disabilities to a person's fault to making it everyone's responsibility to care for the victim.

for everyone. The message was simply this: there's a seat at the table for everyone. David the King has a seat and crippled-feet Mephibosheth has a seat. There was then a run of statements encouraging people to help until the table was filled. Then there was a run of statements encouraging everyone to take their seat at the table so that we could all enjoy the blessings of God the King together as one large unified community. This unification is what enables even the disabled to partake in leadership.

Preaching in the manner described above cancels the contradiction between health and holiness/leadership or being physically lame. It forces each person to know that God's blessings and serving in ministry are open to everyone--not just those without physical limitations. It reverses the emotional stress of trying to fit in or be like others. It removes the need to be "healed" before a person can serve and be an effective leader. This preaching builds a bridge that makes leadership wheelchair accessible, per se. The loud sound of acceptance is communicated at a volume that even the hearing impaired can hear. It gives the senior citizen saint a seat at the ushers' door

Whole Even When Not Healed

right beside the younger saint who stands at the door. This is a form of what Otis Moss calls "Blue Note" preaching. This type of preaching blesses what used to be a contradiction. It presents a God that blesses the handicapped and allows physical disability. This is preaching that sounds like the blues music genre. Pastor Otis Moss refers to this type of preaching when he says,

> *"We view the world in multi-dimensional ways with Blues Speech and a Blues sensibility. We sing songs in major and minor keys and refuse to jettison lament from our vocabulary. The Blues dares us to celebrate all life and find the beauty in the midst of the magnificent mosaic of human contradiction."[21]*

The idea of human contradiction is a necessary message that must be preached to include those who constantly live with issues that others consider reasons to reject them. Those who sing the blues and complain in life must somehow hear from the preacher a message of hope that is opposite of what the majority has impressed upon them. This same idea is expressed by Dr. Frank Thomas when he addresses what he refers to as, "Creative use of reversals." The idea is that

> *"Any preacher who would attend to emotional process must give careful thought to paradox, paradoxical intention, or –the term we prefer– reversals. Reversals are fundamental to human*

life and human communication. The greatest asset of the human mind very well could be its ability to experience paradox."[22]

When we decide to disconnect people from leadership because of their disabilities, we inadvertently cause a disconnect in their relationship with God and the church. That relationship is necessary in order to experience the reign of God. A relationship with God involves more than just hearing a message affirming that God will heal. There are times we must preach that, while you are disabled, God can use you. It may sound disappointing, but this is how reversal works. "Though we automatically and intuitively assume that relationship means non-disappointing behavior, the paradox of disappointing behavior and sustained relationship facilitates fresh encounter."[23] What we will find in this form of Shaky Bridge Preaching is that there is a large segment of people who are tired of hearing about the God who will heal them and are waiting to hear about the God that will accept them as they are. If they must be healed before they can become a leader, they are always denied leadership access. Where is the God who blesses the body that they have? Where is the God who sustains when people get tired of all of the tests, medical trials, and temporary fix procedures? Where is the God who not only favors everyone but every-body? Shaky Bride Preaching elevates that God in front of the congregation for empowerment. There can be preaching about a God who causes Jacob to limp, shuts up the womb of Hannah, and may allow a man to be born blind. But we must not omit preaching scriptures like, "Then the Lord said to him, "Who has made man's mouth? Who makes him mute, or deaf, or seeing, or blind? Is it not I, the Lord? (Exodus 4:11) We must present God as our King like David was their king. Our king will also search for a crippled Mephibosheth with no intent of putting him in a hospital bed for healing but who will, instead, overwhelm him with hospitality and blessing.

Jesus tears the veil to give us all access to God without discrimination!

In the previously mentioned sermon, I pointed out that Ziba made David aware that Mephibosheth was alive but crippled in both feet. David was not concerned about the impairment. In fact, David did not see his crippled feet as a reason to deprive him of this opportunity to be blessed. In this same way, Jesus is the ultimate solution that gives everyone access to the table of leadership. Indeed, Jesus tears the veil to give us all access to God without discrimination and John 14:3 helps us understand the need for this access when Jesus talks about going away to prepare a place where each person will have access to a mansion. This preaching content also includes a type of *physical* prosperity teaching. Debra Mumford alludes to this by asserting,

> *"Prosperity preachers teach their followers that if God made a promise, then God will keep it – even if keeping it seems impossible by human standards. God will keep God's promise because God is faithful and able to do all things."*[24]

Along these lines, I feel that we should encourage the congregation to know God's promises are more about using people as they are rather than having to heal them first. This is an alternative method towards transformation. Ultimately, a sermon that includes a reference to physical prosperity would help solidify the importance of social transformation that, in turn, helps build a connecting bridge.

AUCKLAND HARBOR BRIDGE
AUCKLAND, NEW ZEALAND

RIALTO BRIDGE
VENEZIA, ITALY

Chapter 5

Details in Your Delivery – Control Your Body Language

Change begins with the preacher and is funneled to each leader. This implies that preachers must be willing to change their preaching style. As mentioned earlier, the delivery must match the invitation. For instance, having a redundant style is one mistake made by many preachers that can cause a disconnect. Preaching the same way every single time you speak reduces a person's ability to stay engaged. The less engaged they are the less likely they are to be transformed by the preaching moment. However, by making small alterations to the preaching moment, such as changing movement, weekly messages could begin connecting with a group of worshippers that is normally disengaged. The numerous messages spoken through our body language during preaching can be enhanced so as to create a much more welcoming atmosphere. The more welcoming the preaching moment, the more likely those who have felt far from the preacher in relationship will be drawn to leadership. Building relationships can then motivate those who are distant to become leaders themselves. This can be achieved with the proper use of audible tone, varied voice volumes, hand gestures, and changing from standing behind a podium to moving to the side of a podium. These subtle changes in the preaching moment provide visual images to correlate with the audible message. They also allow lay members to move from knowing what God will do for them to seeing how God has compassion for others. That is, they will begin to feel compassion expressed in body language. Additionally, a simple hand gesture inviting someone to come creates a different emotion than a stern finger pointing in judgment. The actual visual presentation delivered through body language helps people see God through imagery. Fred Craddock puts it this way:

> *"Long after a man's head has consented to the preacher's idea, the old images may still hang in the heart. The longest trip a person takes is that from head to heart. The faith on which people bet their very lives comes not because one has heard and understood a great flow of logical persuasion, though the love of God demands that we understand all we can. Rather, it is the fruit of holistic encounter with familiar images, whatever one's intelligence level."*[25]

Details in Your Delivery

These images are delivered through body language as well as in descriptive preaching. The idea is to know that images are necessary and people are literally looking to hear you. Changing the sermon and text presentation are additional ways to present images that are easily understood. You could also have everyone read the text aloud, display it on a screen, or include some other form of title and text presentation. How we start delivering the message sometimes matters more than what the message is. Therefore, the presentation of the preaching moment must be seriously considered.

> How we start delivering the message sometimes matters more than what the message is.

The way your body feels affects your presentation and determines what people hear. Because of this, there are small but impactful changes you can make to improve and maintain your body's output because it is our whole body--not voice alone--that produces sound. For this reason, stretching your muscles prior to sermon delivery could be of great help. That is, preachers should consider beginning the preaching process by relaxing and stretching the muscles that are going to be used in delivering God's message. This used to be difficult for me; however, it has now become a normal part of my preaching process.

In her book, *Freeing the Natural Voice,* Kristen Linklater mentions that, "It may be hard to prevent your muscles from helping to make the sound at this point."[26] At first, I did not know exactly what she meant, but I figured I should stretch to make this moment easier. Linklater was right. It is difficult to control my sounds when I have not stretched, but afterwards it is different. By engaging in facial stretching, muscle tension release, and draw dropping exercises before preaching, I can now mount the pulpit ready to experience God through sermon delivery. And for any preacher desiring to make a change in delivery and/or wanting to be intentional about engaging the congregation, I suggest this same (or a similar) regimen. By doing so, those to whom you are preaching will not just hear the sermon but, rather, experience the transforming power of God to raise them into leadership. You are probably laughing at the idea of facial stretching. I would ask you to remember our opening conversation about being open to change. I would suggest you try it before totally dismissing it. If nothing else, it will provide an awareness about how the preaching moment goes beyond your carefully crafted verbiage and extends to your body language.

Another element of style change in preaching is scripture reading. In many traditions, it is the preacher alone who has the privilege of reading the text aloud. As mentioned above, this could be a place where you instantly engage listeners by switching it from time to time. Keeping in this tradition, it was

Details in Your Delivery

second nature for me to simply read the scripture aloud to all of those in attendance. However, I've come to understand that when the congregation is invited to share in the reading they also share in the intimacy of the moment with God. With this in mind, on one occasion, I added an element of corporate reading of the sacred text. I did this based on the notion that *who* reads scripture may affect to whom and how it is received. When the entire congregation is asked to read one of the verses from the chosen text together, it may help them identify with what has been deemed priority in the text. Childers puts it this way, "It is the preacher's job to make some decisions about which piece of the text deserves priority, which aspects of the text should be divided from each other, and which are important to keep linked."[27] Moreover, "the worship service answers these questions these conflicts pose – from "Am I saved or am I damned?...conflict between who God is and whom we know ourselves to be..."[28] When the congregant is afforded the opportunity to read the focus scripture, in some ways, it makes them the preacher for a moment. This moment empowers them and they have a chance to lead themselves. Since introducing the method of

> When the congregant is afforded the opportunity to read the focus scripture, in some ways, it makes them the preacher for a moment.

having parishioners read scripture aloud instead of simply reading it silently to themselves, I've found that it lets the listener experience God personally. I've also found that this method causes the prioritized scripture, and the sermon itself, to resonate greater. This discovery was the beginning of a different type of delivery.

The presentation of a personal backstory in the introduction of a sermon is yet another element of change that impacts sermon presentation and reception. This differs from a typical metaphor or analogy that may have little to no realism. Instead, it is the inclusion of a story that is true about the preacher but, at the same time, not too revealing. I've wrestled with this concept and was finally released when remembering how freeing it was during one of the classes in my doctoral studies. In *God's Human Speech*, by Charles Bartow, he states, "It is important to 'paint people into the scenes' of the encounter of the biblical world with the world of the preacher, and there let people discover for themselves how they feel and what, if anything, they feel they must do."[29] I've found this to be true and when retelling stories of my class time, others were in awe of how effective they believed the power of testimony could be. They found an even greater connection when I used it during this sermon. I now recommend it as a necessity in transforming laity into leaders. There's something about the personal testimony that allows people to see themselves in the sacred text.

MILLAU VIADUCT
AVEYRON, FRANCE

GATESHEAD MILLENNIUM BRIDGE
NEWCASTLE, UK

CHAPTER 6

CONNECT THE NARRATIVES – NEW SOUND TO AN OLD STORY

Seeing oneself as living in the Bible is paramount to living out biblical principles. If we want laity to become leaders outside of the Bible, we must help them see themselves as leaders within the pages of the Bible. The age-old verse by verse explanation of the Gospel was good for a time period, but it may not be as effective in today's time as the only preaching style for transformation. The retelling of the Gospel in story form has the potential to embed the Gospel and love of Jesus into the hearts of those who may have missed this same message due to the rigidity of the sermon structure. Storytelling during the preaching moment allows the listener to hear main ideas that are intentionally inserted, but it also allows listeners to form their own opinions and lessons. This increased participation in the preaching moment can result in the desire to increase participation in organizations overall. To hear that the events of a single biblical story have taken place in many other biblical stories and in our own lives creates a personal connection to the text. When the preaching moment becomes personal so does the organization in which we serve. People build connections to the place because it's where they hear about themselves. When our church, community, and workplace are more than just places we go, we are much more likely to serve in them. Storytelling provides a personal touch that inspires a person to want to personally touch lives as leaders.

> Storytelling provides a personal touch that inspires a person to want to personally touch lives as leaders.

I really enjoyed what Dr. Joy Moore calls, "the threading of the Hebrew narrative throughout the text." This entails the weaving of many stories into one story and it is a way to help laity place themselves in one of many narratives being presented simultaneously. If when preaching a sermon there is a question as to how many stories are appropriate to overlap in a single presentation of the Gospel, a preacher could simply apply Sachs' "Story Test" and examine the "broadcast era's five deadly sins."[30] The following Story Tests can be used to evaluate the effectiveness of the message and also to indicate whether or not a story is good or bad:

Trial of Vanity: Bad if the story is all about you, yours, and your brand, but good if the stories highlights how great others are and particularly if it's the listening audience being celebrated

Trial of Authority: Bad if you only use data and expertise, but good if you create characters that build emotions and allow for an experience that makes us believe the facts

Trial of Insincerity: Bad if you only say what you think you want to hear, but good if you share the story behind why you think what you do and allow others to share in the process

Trial of Puffery: Bad if you are using God's voice to command the audience to act, but good if you are using a human voice to inspire each person to use their gifts

Trial of Gimmickry: Bad if you are inciting temporarily quick emotional reactions, but good if you are building real emotions centered around common values with humor as the foundation

These test questions will help develop the right content when using multiple stories in any given presentation. The mention of multiple biblical narratives happening at once creates tension in the text that is very difficult to ignore. This textual tension is easily connected to the life of laity because there are numerous characters from varied narratives with whom they can identify. I found this more than captivating when preaching 1 Chronicles 28:1-11.

During the narrative of this text, Solomon appears and is told what he must do. It seems that whatever plans he had for his life are disregarded as David's desire to build a temple is now thrust upon him. In that text, God is speaking to David about his selection of Solomon to build the temple and this would be an interruption of Solomon's personal plans so that God can use him to bless a larger group of people. This not only served as the main tension of the text, but it was also a place where I presented multiple narratives woven within the one sermon text. I attempted to season the sermon with Godly revelation hoping to discover a meaningful thread. This moment in the sermon for me was the epitome of "Storied Worlds", a concept mentioned by Jonah Sachs. Storied Worlds is an idea that there are no new stories, i.e. we often just retell the same stories in different forms. For example, most Disney stories tell the same story. There is a princess, a prince, a villain and before it is over the prince defeats the villain and saves the princess. This is a common story told simply through various characters in different tales.

This is what I attempted to do in the sermon believing that it would be a way to bridge gaps and create a familiarity between an ancient text and present day events. I shared additional biblical narratives that show how God often interrupts

Connect the Narratives

personal plans for a greater cause. These stories and thread began with Esther, spoke of Jonah, added Jeremiah, and referenced Job. All of them have moments of interruption that I mentioned as common to us all. It was presenting the Storied Worlds. I then made a transition to a media and movie list beginning with *The Lion King*. This transition is where the threading has its best effect.

The Lion King was one movie that I used to build an entire textual parallel. It made one connection between the text and our lives with the single movie. In this movie, Simba's life was interrupted with his kingly father's plans. I felt this was a great idea because the goal was to lift listeners from their pews and place them in the story. Paul Wilson says the sermon *"...is not writing an essay. We are taking listeners into the world of the text."*[31] I then extended the idea and instead of just using one movie I showed the similarity between the text and numerous movies and television shows from multiple genres and multiple time frames. I wanted to allow God to speak while keeping this idea presented by Cleophas LaRue in mind:

> The only thing that should take precedence over openness to the imagination is our openness to the Spirit.

> *"The only thing that should take precedence over openness to the imagination is our*

> *openness to the Spirit. And just as this openness to the movement of the spirit cannot be assumed but rather eagerly sought and accepted on its own terms, so too, the imagination."*[32]

I attempted to use older media and current media from multiple viewing categories. While I must be honest and admit that *The Lion King* is my favorite movie by far, I did not want to avoid reaching the young generation that now enjoys *The Lion Guard* (featuring Kion who is Simba's son) in place of *The Lion King* (featuring Mufasa and Simba). I also did not want to miss connecting to a more mature crowd that would not have known either of these animated films. Here is where I remembered how learning of the biblical parallels to *The Hunger Games* discussed during my doctoral residency allowed me to better view the biblical text.

I sought to find the Solomon thread in the older animated *Lion King* and also in the newly released and wildly popular Disney movie *Frozen* with Elsa and Ana. I used the interruption in a classic American movie *(The Wizard of Oz)* and a classic African American film *(Coming to America)* and mentioned a recently released movie starring Will Smith entitled *Suicide Squad*. I connected to a young adult group with popular weeknight TV shows such as *Empire* and *Power* that are favorites among young adults. For those who were not pop culture enthusiasts, but may have been keeping up with the heated and controversial political campaign, I ended the thread by showing the interruption in our political plans with the unlikely selection of the two current presidential nominees at that time. The goal was not only to thread through the Bible or just one movie but to thread this "Solomon tension" up and down every pew in the sanctuary and somehow get the message to resonate with every person regardless of his/her preferred media outlet(s). In every example listed, there had been interruptions. The interruptions that listeners had vicariously experienced via entertainment were now being compared to the interruptions in their lives and in the text. This is Shaky Bridge Preaching at its best-- one moment in a sermon connecting all aspects of our world.

The goal was achieved then and should be attempted now by preachers truly seeking transformation in their pews. The audible responses during the preaching moment seemed to confirm this along with the many comments after the preaching moment. Many approached me referencing which show or movie they had seen and how their life was very much like the characters mentioned in the movie. While this has not been the goal of traditional preaching, it is effective and it achieves the goal. I will be honest and admit that it has not been the norm for me. I have failed so many times at trying to connect the ancient text to this modern world. I had a Gutenberg Press "just say what happened in the text and only talk about the text" type of mentality because of the traditional preaching under which I was reared. Leonard Sweet once said,

> "As we have seen, a 'head first' Gutenberg world dismissed emotions in favor of intellect. But the greatest communicators in history have been those who had the ability to turn thoughts into emotions that move peoples and nations. Good scholars have the power of concentrating a world of intense thought into a single image or phrase a world of . Good poets have the power of concentrating into a single image or phrase a world of intense feeling. Great preachers have a power of concentrating into a single image or story an intense world of thought and feeling."[33]

> **Transformation from laity to leadership can occur because the listener is given an opportunity to connect with any part of the message and not just the part(s) the preacher deems as a priority.**

Traditional preaching would have found success in a person relating to the biblical character and not the movie or television actor. This is where change in the preacher must take place. Transformation from laity to leadership can occur because the listener is given an opportunity to connect with any part of the message and not just the part(s)

Connect the Narratives

the preacher deems as a priority. In the sermon account above, I would have loved for everyone to see themselves as Solomon; however, if someone walked away feeling like Mufasa, then hearing them roar when they had previously been lamb-like would have been a great God-sized accomplishment.

As I reflect on that preaching moment, I can see that this accomplishment was reached after connecting each person to the problem in the text and then presenting the grace of God to solve that same problem. What this indicates is that preachers should not leave people doubting, or feeling as if their plans are worthless; but, instead, they should inspire them with the knowledge that God cares. What looks out of place to us is still something that is Divinely inspired. David Lose says this:

> **What looks out of place to us is still something that is Divinely inspired.**

"Whether they know it or not, the loss of hope so many of our people and leaders express is a characteristic not just of the church but of the larger secular age in which the church exist. For if, as we've already discussed, postmodernity represents a loss of confidence in modernism's optimism about human reason and progress, secularism represents a loss of confidence not in human things, but divine."[34]

This helps us to understand that our hope should not be focused so much on *our actions* but, rather, on *God's divinity* in the process.

This can be a daunting task. So after spending time connecting each person to the tension, there should be an attempt to lead the listener back into the grace of God. Lead them to the knowledge that Jesus was a part of the biblical story as well as our life stories today. If Stackhouse and Crisp are right when they say, "... preaching an Old Testament narrative text resembles climbing Mount Everest...Getting to the summit is the easy part; it's getting back down that's hard"[35] and "The difficulty preachers face is proclaiming the prophetic challenge in a sermon that is gospel-centered and points listeners to Christ."[36] Then the overall message will show both individuals and God in the same place. The message of the sermon I described earlier in this chapter was about life bringing interruptions, but any inclusion of multiple narratives within a sermon will provide a brief interruption to boredom and disconnection that can end in disengaged laity. I contend that you can find transformation when the preacher adds variety in storytelling to connect more people to a God who became flesh to connect with us.

BIXBY CREEK BRIDGE
BIG SUR, CALIFORNIA

SYDNEY HARBOR BRIDGE
SYDNEY, AUSTRALIA

CHAPTER 7

COMFORT IN CHANGE – CROSSING THE BRIDGE

The major premise of this book so far has been that preaching is a "shaky bridge." It is given this parallel because experiencing change, while necessary, is not always easy. Shaky Bridge Preaching creates a somewhat unsettling terrain for many that are experiencing it; but, in order to transform laity into leaders, our preaching must address change. This approach may not be common or comfortable, but it is necessary. There should be some intentional preaching on how to handle change. This type of preaching, where the focus is on the various aspects of change, will be helpful in reducing the shock factor that typically occurs when people are prompted to change. It will also help prevent a greater divide among the congregation if the effects of change are not addressed. People need to know what to expect when change occurs. However, when a call to change is proclaimed from the pulpit with scriptural authenticity, current and emerging leaders are able to merge together successfully thus proving that preaching is indeed a catalytic bridge that transforms laity into leaders and enhances the body of Christ.

Laura Lundblad, in her book *Transforming the Stone: Preaching Through Resistance to Change*, presents a very convincing case of how preaching can bring transformation. She refers to the old methods, ideals, and traditions as stones and argues that, "For people of faith, transformation doesn't happen: it is a gift from God."[37] If in fact transformation is a gift from God, it will take the preached word of God to usher in that transformation. Change must be preached.

> **Change must be preached!**

To maximize effectiveness during the preaching moment, there could be a place where change is both identified and examined even if the preacher is uncertain about how this new leadership in church, community, and workplace will look. Tim Sensing, in his article "The Art of Asking a Question" says, *"If you want your art to appear somewhere other than your refrigerator door, then do not assume expertise."*[38] The same is true of change in leadership. The preacher does not have to know exactly what the product of change will be. The preacher does not have to paint a perfect portrait of this new leadership lifestyle. There should be honest inclusion of trouble/triumph and good days/bad days. These challenges can be presented when change is identified in the text. The sermon should also show Alexandar

Grashow's (senior advisor to Cambridge Leadership Associates and a leading expert on change theory) problem solving approaches of observation, interpretation, and intervention in a way that helps laity learn and apply it in their everyday lives. Just as it's presented in the text, change can be difficult in our organizations. Moreover, the preacher should also show biblical illustrations of leaders both asking and answering the questions often asked by Gil Rendle and Alice Mann such as, "Who are we? What has God called us to do or be? Who is our neighbor?"[39] These questions are simple but critical in encouraging people to cross the bridge towards change. When questions like these are presented and answered during the preaching moment, they reinforce the idea that the challenges of change can be overcome and, thus, present a realistic perspective of what the transformation from laity into leadership will look and feel like.

Presenting this perspective is necessary so that laity will not be discouraged during the transition. The more informed a person is about the trials of transition the more prepared they will be to endure the process. "Transformational preaching is more than demythologizing and deconstructing. Testing what is written in stone doesn't mean the erosion of all we have received from the past."[40] When embracing transformation, there is a shared sense of holding on to what has been while making the leap across the bridge of challenge into the new model of leadership. Change can take place and it does not have to be viewed or received as a threat when it is prompted by preaching. The end goal is that no person has to live a life that is limited to their current place. This change proclaims, "We should all be liberated!" James Cone wrote, "The history of Israel is a history of God's election of a special, oppressed people to share in his creative involvement in the world on behalf of man."[41] Dr. James Harris comments on that same idea by saying, "Cone makes it clear that the church, in order to be authentic, has to participate in the activity of human liberation."[42] The change that comes through preaching will liberate both laity and leaders to fully embrace God's call to the church at large. Shaky Bridge Preaching is the church's participation in changing human chains into human opportunity.

> Shaky Bridge Preaching is the church's participation in changing human chains into human opportunity.

UNIVERSITY OF RICHMOND - WESTHAMPTON LAKE BRIDGE
RICHMOND, VA

EDITH CARRIER ARBORETUM BRIDGE
HARRISONBURG, VA

Chapter 8

Personal Testimonies – After the Bridge is Built

My hope is that, by now, you better understand how Shaky Bridge Preaching, coupled with a balance of the previously mentioned methods, can enable the transition of laity into leaders. My personal experience with these methods and my encounter with laity who have made that transition make me confident that, when properly applied, Shaky Bridge Preaching can indeed become the catalyst for transformation. I have seen it take place in my congregation as I've listened to and watched our congregation evolve. I must admit, however, that the transformation was not necessarily easy to predict or manage; it was without a doubt "shaky ground." Still, although shaky, people moved from being laid back laity to out front leaders. I have watched many who once let life's setbacks make them feel less qualified than others rise to leadership roles and pursue promotions on their jobs. I have even had conversations about seeking city office positions with members that I had not considered for leadership roles in our church.

In the beginning, preaching from the bridge building angle provided an entirely new style of sermonic presentation. This preaching style was discussed with a small group of randomly selected members and our associate preachers. They would approach me after service and during the week with tons of questions about the sermon structure, format, and delivery style. It was uncommon to their ear but touching to their lives. This caused me to redesign our preaching classes. They would say things like, "Pastor I don't know what you were doing, or which style you were using, but I've never heard it put like that before. You made me feel like I could do more and better." These types of comments are the statements that signaled individual growth and a leaning towards leadership. They are also what caused me to reconsider whether or not I had been the one holding back my congregation. Along these lines, one idea that permeated my thoughts was perhaps it had been my negligence, like those who should have been caring for Shaky Bridge in New Zealand, that dissuaded lay members from pursuing leadership. I then took serious evaluation of myself and discovered

> **Preaching from the bridge building angle provided an entirely new style of sermonic presentation.**

Personal Testimonies

that it is just as much my job to preach hope to the hopeless and salvation to the lost as it is to spark a desire in laity to pursue leadership. Once I committed to bridge building through preaching, the transformation was almost immediate. It was as if people who had been caged in were awaiting an opportunity to bolt into leadership.

In case you're wondering, Shaky Bridge Preaching worked very well for our congregation. I found this to be especially true with regard to one of the most eye opening transformations in our church—the rise of disabled, impaired, and chronically ill members that took place in response to the Mephibosheth sermon. Since that message, and the study that followed, our congregation now has two partially paralyzed members serving in ministry, one hearing impaired worshipper who helps write grants for our community empowerment center, and an arm amputee who has joined both our men's and media ministries. In addition, we have had three members with multiple sclerosis share their testimonies and join our health ministry.

We have also had several members become paralyzed or confined to wheelchairs over the past twelve years but it is my goal to help others accept them as valuable and necessary in each ministry. As Lundblad states, "It's critical to help people see that change does not mean erosion of the faith or the destruction of deep values."[43] In the Mephibosheth sermon, establishing early on that everyone deserves a seat at the table revealed more people than I ever knew who were either ashamed or angry because of their conditions. They had previously put their faith in God the healer and not a God that uses the disabled. This sermon ignited a change in their theology and involvement in ministry. An example of this is Eulinda, a member of our congregation who is partially paralyzed on one side of her body and walks with a cane. She joined our Greeters Ministry. Typically, the greeters stand at the outside doors and welcome our new members and current members with hugs and smiles.

> It's critical to help people see that change does not mean erosion of the faith or the destruction of deep values.

Embarrassingly, given these facets of the ministry and her disability, I had never considered her for this ministry. So, it was to my surprise that the Sunday following the sermon, Eulinda joined and had a seat right near the front door. She smiled big, and I smiled when I saw her, and then she exclaimed, "Pastor, I'm taking my seat at the table!" Weeks later I received a report from the greeters ministry leader stating that Eulinda joining their ministry had tremendously turned things around. It turned out that not only was she smiling in her seat at the door, but she was also an administrative genius who organized all of our new member cards, sent immediate follow up calls, and documented how many of them came back to worship. She even tracked whether they had been missing. She noted that she knew what it felt like to miss a Sunday then return and no one know that she had been missing. She was connecting with others who had been overlooked in a way the other leaders and I had never thought to. While she may not have been able to move as fast as others on her feet, her mind was as swift as an Olympic Gold Medalist during a 100 yard dash. She had transformed. She had transformed us.

> We melt and are formed into something new, but the burned bits remain.

What made it shaky for others was finally coming to grips with the fact that a person who only had movement on one side of her body had somehow connected with people they were never able to. She was doing more than our current leaders with less physical ability. Some questioned her longevity and stamina--both physically and administratively. They wondered aloud about things such as if she would record information correctly (which was never an issue). Ultimately, despite her great work, they were still standing on a shaky bridge waiting for the breakdown. However, I am happy to report that she is still efficient, still presenting new ideas, and still in her seat at the table of leadership and has shown no form of deficiency in her ministry production.

Similar to her story, that same sermon moved members of our leadership after we studied everyone having a seat at the table. Our leaders realized that we had not adequately accommodated those who may be impaired, handicapped, or disabled. I watched our leaders voluntarily build a closet space to hold walkers and folded wheelchairs, type song lyrics on the screen for the hearing impaired, and assign an extra usher near the elevator for those requiring assistance to the most convenient seats in the sanctuary. Even our current leaders have taken a step out onto the shaky bridge. They have risked their current places to venture into other iterations of leadership. I do not believe that these actions were accidental or coincidental. These changes happened after the preaching.

Shaky Bridge Preaching was the catalyst that sparked the transformation of current leaders into better leaders. They did not have to lose themselves but, instead, they took their not so great areas and made them better. It is what Pastor Nadia Bolz-Weber refers to when she tells the story of how her church reburns candles. In her church, *The House For All Sinners and Saints*, they use last year's wax to make this year's candles. And each year when they burn, she parallels the candles to our lives when she says, "We melt and are formed into something new, but the burned bits remains."[44] This is a great example of the transformation I saw in our leaders. They morphed

Personal Testimonies

into new candles in their leadership roles while their core remained the same.

Greater still, our church has even experienced a rise in participation from our senior members. A notable example of this took place after I delivered a message on Nehemiah during a Wednesday night worship experience. Upon the conclusion of the service, this overlooked population decided that although they could not function the way they used to function, they were still valuable and could serve others who may be less capable than themselves. Since that week, they now serve meals, visit the sick, and volunteer in our church office during the week.

Another change worth noting happened with our current leaders. Our church has had the distinction of having many professionals lead our ministries. While that used to be a reason to celebrate, the dynamics of who leads has also been shaking up for more inclusion which is something even greater to celebrate. In recent years, we have had more than ten men join our ministry after returning home from incarceration in response to Shaky Bridge Preaching. Additionally, not only have two of them acknowledged their call to preach during this time, but six of them have acquired jobs and sought promotions. Prior to the introduction of Shaky Bridge Preaching, they would simply sit at home, frustrated, and would

> **We are walking by faith across a shaky bridge.**

often use their past incarceration as an excuse for why they were unable to find work. But, the constant emphasis on everyone being qualified—despite fallacies and "people's" judgment—inspired them, catapulted their self-esteem, and drove them to ambitiously apply for employment positions for

> Your ministry has the potential to change lives in wonderful ways. Give God your all by taking advantage of the resources available to empower you.

which, on paper, they were under qualified. While all of them have not yet been employed, they all took pride in applying and a couple of them have begun leadership training. This illustrates the very important point that transformation is not proven in getting a certain position—be it in church or in the marketplace—but, rather, it is in starting the journey across the bridge towards the position.

The last, but definitely not least, transformation I saw was the transformation in me. That's right. I, the preacher and bridge builder, have changed. I can also testify that this preaching is indeed a shaky bridge because for the first time in my seventeen years of ministry I am comfortably standing on shaky ground. Did you read that slow enough to really grasp the feeling? I am comfortable while in a very shaky place. I can rarely predict exactly what is going to happen or who is going to emerge from the rear and assist. My church and I are in a place where the only constant is change and the only certainty is insecurity. Furthermore, all that we once deemed as productive has been replaced with the very things we once felt would create panic because these latter things work. It is in this new place, suspended on a shaky bridge, that we all are finding comfort. We are walking by faith across a shaky bridge. I am leading laity and current leaders across a shaky bridge. We have experienced sound preaching on a shaky bridge.

I was in unchartered territory personally with Shaky Bridge Preaching. This is especially true with my sermon preparation. I used to cherish the private moments I had when preparing sermons. These times were moderately reserved during the week and greatly reserved on the weekends just between God and me. Now, my sermon preparation time is often shared with an extended small group that makes up a preaching team. I still get the last say and opportunity to abide with God alone, but sharing has become beneficial. Each week in between our 8:30 early morning and 11:00 worship services, I meet with this mixed group of associate preachers and laity to discuss the sermon that was just preached. I even meet with them weeks or days before the sermon to gather their insights and critique. Their responses are totally different from other trained homileticians or neighboring preachers. They give feedback that represents the listeners. I then amend the message based on the input of the group.

In the past, this would have never been included in my preaching process; however, I now better realize what Adam Bond meant when he said, "Your ministry has the potential to change lives in wonderful ways. Give God your all by taking advantage of the resources available to empower you."[45] This means more than just books and internet resources. And while I have always been a person who notes others' potential, I now know there have been overlooked resources sitting in the pews waiting to be invited to the table of sermon preparation. Each person in the group is a resource. Including them in the sermon preparation is a trip across a bridge most of them never expected to take. To be honest, I don't think I ever imagined inviting anyone across that bridge into the sermonic moment. However, having traveling partners in sermon prep has been one of the best journeys I've made.

The testimonies and examples shared above are just a few ways I have personally seen how Shaky Bridge Preaching brings transformation and enhances organizations to benefit the entire body of Christ. The emergence of new leaders provides a variety of both the personality and perspective of God's Spirit that currently does not exist in various segments of society. Furthermore, a broader variety is essential to any organization's growth so that it is not limited to any one market or type of personalities.

Personal Testimonies

Ultimately, because people come in a myriad of shapes, sizes, theologies, ideals, and cultural practices, and since the goal is to bring transformation to the entire organization, we must appeal to each type of person. As Lundblad puts it:

> *"Common ground will differ from one congregation to another. There are also differences within a congregation: people may be at very different places in talking about sexuality, in their feelings about family, and in their interpretation of the Bible. Listening to these different voices is critically important. It will be almost impossible for people to reconsider long-held values if they feel they have been disregarded or dismissed."*[46]

And since the goal is to bring transformation to the entire organization, we must appeal to each type of person. To accomplish this most important task, it is incumbent upon us, the proclaimers of the Gospel, to be intentional about targeting our sermons in order for preaching to truly be a catalyst that transforms laity into leaders in the church, community, and marketplace.

Indeed, Bridge Preaching has opened my eyes to people I had overlooked. I literally see people in our congregation differently. I see everyone as a potential leader without the requirement of completing leadership courses or being involved in our church for a set period of time. I must admit that I rarely know the outcome of each person's involvement, but that is what makes it shaky. So far, the shaky bridge has allowed many lay members to pursue leadership and they have contributed to our church, community, and marketplace in ways we had not expected. The shaky bridge has also moved us to adopt new theologies in numerous areas of our church. While Lundblad is right that, "...new ways of doing theology are not always welcomed,"[47] we have found that, welcomed or not, it is our new norm. Moreover, I am a witness for how sound preaching that produces a shaky bridge can transform laity into leaders in the church, community, and marketplace. I now encourage you to maximize your potential. Go build a bridge.

> The shaky bridge has allowed many lay members to pursue leadership and they have contributed to our church, community, and marketplace in ways we had not expected.

TOWER BRIDGE
TOWER BRIDGE, LONDON

KHAJU BRIDGE
ISHAFAN, IRAN

Appendix

About this Book - Cover Information

The cover was designed by Evelina Johnson-Beundia. The iPad has a list of scriptures noting the importance of preaching. The Scripture referred to on the Bible is Hebrews 13. There are many lessons learned when this text is read from the framework of preaching. The notebook has the original sketches that were used when envisioning how preaching serves as a shaky bridge. The use of technology and hardcopy text is intentional as I hope the principles in this book transcend time and travel from generation to generation with each media form. Lastly, nestled in the bridge sketch you will find both a crown and an M. This has been a symbol representing Crowned Ministries International, a college ministry (now life coaching organization) founded at JMU, that prides itself on helping each person maximize their potential. Take a look at the cover again, Shaky Bridge Preaching begins there.

About The Bridge Photographs

Preface – These Bridges are of the actual Shaky Bridge in New Zealand that is used in the metaphor for preaching.

Chapter 1 – The Chaban bridge lifts and lowers to allow passengers to cross, while the Charles Bridge is always open for travel. These represent the goal of the bridge keeper. We must allow for constantly flow across our bridges.

Chapter 2 – The Brooklyn Bridge is an icon and the Bridge of America is in Panama. These represent how preaching can be local and global.

Chapter 3 – The Garden bridge works and is small. However, the Golden Gate bridge is much larger. This is an illustration of how people can grow if grace is applied.

Chapter 4 – Both of these bridges are missing planks, however, they are still bridges. In the same way, those that are disabled may not be as physically active but they can still lead.

Chapter 5 – These two bridges have stone foundations that keep them sturdy. The body is our foundation for communication and serves as the premier form of transformation.

Chapter 6 – Did you notice how unique these bridges are? They are not normally designed bridges, however, the change in their design does not make them any less effective. They are proof that change is not bad.

Chapter 7 – The bridges pictured here are both long. Becoming comfortable with change is not a short process; it, too, is long. Build the bridge with endurance.

Chapter 8 – These are bridges that can be found on the undergraduate college campuses of my wife and me. They are very familiar and carry many memories. The testimonies I have as a result of Shaky Bridge Preaching are also great memories that we as a family share.

Appendix – Thick stone bridges supply support. The information beyond this chapter presents all of the authors that support this writing via their own books and teachings.

About The Author

Dr. Dwight Shawrod Riddick, II was reared in Hampton, VA. He enjoys meeting and learning from diverse people. With a passion for teaching, empowering, and training, D. Shawrod Riddick, II uses his unique gift of bridging gaps between cultures to maximize the potential of those around him. He is the husband of Jennell Whitfield and they are the proud parents of Dwight III and Jasmine.

As a product of Hampton City Schools in Hampton, VA, he graduated from Phoebus High School with honors, earned a Bachelor of Science degree in Computer Science as a lettered student athlete (basketball) at James Madison University (JMU), an M. Div from Virginia Union University, a Doctorate in Homiletics from Chicago Theological Seminary, and is a certified John Maxwell Leadership Coach. He is humbled to have been chosen as a Styberg Preaching Peer Group Facilitator at Garrett Theological Seminary at Northwestern University.

While attending JMU, he became one of the six founders of JMU Impact Movement, a minority ministry affiliated with the International Ministry Campus Crusade for Christ. He served as the campus ministry leader and founder of a spirit led and growing ministry named Crowned Ministries International (CMI). CMI was founded to maximize the potential of youth and young adults on multiple college and high school campuses. He honed his ministry skills as the youth and young adult Pastor at Gethsemane Baptist

Church in Newport News, VA. Since Christmas 2005, he has been privileged to serve as the Senior Pastor of First Baptist Church in Franklin, VA.

Dr. Riddick also serves as an adjunct professor at Paul D. Camp Community College in Suffolk, VA as a religion instructor and is a proud and active member of Alpha Phi Alpha Fraternity Incorporated. As a published author, he mentors and provides both leadership and life coaching as a founding member of Crowned Ministries International Leadership Coaching (CMI-LC Inc). This group uses a customized curriculum authorized by John Maxwell. You can learn more by visiting www.cmileadershipcoach.com.

Standing on the word of God as stated in Philippians 2:14 which says, "Do everything without complaining or arguing," and Philippians 4:11 which states, "...I have learned the secret of being content in any and every situation..." Dr. Riddick says that God has been too good to him for him to complain. So he is dedicated to helping others maximize their potential while on their mission to see Jesus. Stay connected at www.dsriddick.com or by following @dsriddick2 on Facebook, Instagram, or Twitter.

Bibliography

Allen, Ronald. *Patterns of Preaching: A Sermon Sampler*. St. Louis, MO: Chalice Press, 1998.

Augsburger, David. *Pastoral Counseling across Cultures*. Louisville, KY. Westminster John Knox Press. 1986.

Bartow, Charles L. *God's Human Speech: A Practical Theology of Proclamation*. Grand Rapids, MI, Eerdmans. 1997.

Brooks, Gennifer. *Good News Preaching: Offering the Gospel in Every Sermon*. Cleveland, OH: Pilgrim Press, 2009.

Buechner, Frederick. *Telling the Truth: The Gospel as Tragedy, Comedy, and Fairy Tale*. New York City, NY. Harper & Row, 1977.

Buller, Cornelius A. "Healing Hope: Physical Healing and Resurrection Hope in a Postmodern Context." Journal of Pentecostal Theology 10 (2002): 74-92.

Cone, James. The White Church and Black Power: In Black Theology: A Documentary History, ed. Wilmore and Cone.

Cosgrove, Charles, and Dow Edgerton. *In Other Words. Incarnational Translation for Preaching.* Grand Rapids, MI: Eerdmans, 2007.

Childers, Jana. *Performing The Word: Preaching As Theatre.* Nashville, TN. Abingdon Press, 1998.

Crowder, Stephanie. *When Momma Speaks: The Bible and Motherhood from a Womanist Perspective.* Lousville, KY. Westminister John Knox Press, 2016

Fabarez, John. *Preaching that Changes Lives.* Eugene, OR: Wipf & Stock, 2005.

Harris, James. *Pastoral Theology: A Black Church Perspective.* Minneapolis, MN. Fortress Press, 1991

Hoezee, Scott. *Actuality: Real Life Stories for Sermons that Matter.* Nashville, TN. Abingdon Press, 2014.

Hogan, Lucy. *Graceful Speech. An Invitation to Preaching.* Louisville, KY. Westminster John Knox Press, 2006.

Jensen, Richard. *Thinking in Story: Preaching in A Post-literate Age.* Lima, OH. CSS Publishing Co., 1995.

Kim, Eunjoo Mary. *Preaching in an Age of Globalization.* Louisville, KY. Westminster John Knox Press, 2010. Kindle.

Kim, Eunjoo Mary, and Deborah Beth Creamer. *Women, Church, and Leadership*. Eugene, OR: Pickwick Publications, 2012.

LaRue, Cleophas J. *I Believe I'll Testify: The Art of African American Preaching*. Louisville, KY. Westminster John Knox, 2011.

Linklater, Kristen. *Freeing the Natural Voice*. New York, NY. Drama Book Publishers, 2006.

Linklater, Kristin. *The Divine Voice: Christian Proclamation and the Theology of Sound*. Ada, MI. Brazos Press, 2004.

Long, Thomas. *The Witness of Preaching*. 2nd ed. Louisville, KY. Westminster John Knox Press, 2005.

Lose, David J. *Preaching at the Crossroads: How the World – And Our Preaching – Is Changing*. Minneapolis, MN. Fortress Press, 2013.

Lose, David. *Preaching at the Crossroads. How the World and our Preaching is Changing*. Minneapolis, MN. Fortress Press, 2013.

Lundblad, Barbara K. *Transforming the Stone: Preaching Through Resistance to Change*. Nashville, TN. Abingdon Press, 2001.

McClure, John S. *Other-wise Preaching: A Postmodern Ethic for Homiletics*. St. Louis, MO. Chalice Press, 2001.

McKenzie, Alyce. *Novel Preaching. Tips from Top Writers on Crafting Creative Sermons*.

Louisville: Westminster John Knox Press, 2010.

Mitchell, Henry. *Celebration and Experience in Preaching*. Nashville, TN. Abingdon Press, 2008.

Moss, Otis, III. *Blue Note Preaching in a Post-Soul World: Finding Hope in an Age of Despair*. Louisville: Westminster John Knox, 2015.

Mumford, Debra J. *The Reign of God: A Holistic Vision of Human Health*. Louisville, KY. Louisville Presbyterian Theological Seminary, 2008.

Mumford, Debra J. *Exploring Prosperity Preaching: Biblical Health, Wealth, and Wisdom*. Valley Forge, PA: Judson Press, 2012.

Rendle, Gil and Mann, Alice. *Holy Conversations: Strategic Planning as a Spiritual Practice for Congregations*. Rowman & Littlefield Publishers. 2003

Riddick, Dwight S Sr. *Does Preaching Have a Future. A Call to Join the Conversation*. Bloomington, IN: Universe, 2015.

Sachs, Jonah, *Winning the Story Wars: Why Those Who Tell – and Live – the Best Stories Will Rule the Future*. Cambridge, MA: Harvard Business Review Press, 2012.

Sensing, Tim. *Qualitative Reasearch: A Multi-Methods Approach to Projects for Doctor of Ministry Theses*. Wipf & Stock Pub. 2011.

Stackhouse, Ian, and Oliver D. Crisp. *Text Message: The Centrality of Scripture in Preaching.* Eugene, OR: Pickwick Publications, 2014.

Sweet, Leonard. *Giving Blood: A Fresh Paradigm for Preaching.* Grand Rapid, MI. Zondervan, 2014.

Tanner, Kathryn. *Theories of Culture. A New Agenda For Theology.* Minneapolis, MN. Fortress Press, 1997.

Thomas. Frank. *They Liked to Never Quit Praisin' God. The Role of Celebration in Preaching.* Cleveland, OH. Pilgrim Press, 2013.

Townes, Emile. *In a Blaze of Glory: Womanist Spirituality as Social Witness.* Nashville: Abingdon Press, 1995.

Watson, Lance. *That Was Then - This is Now: Properly Packaging Your Past.* Richmond, VA. Forward Media and Publishing. 2013.

Wilson, Paul. *The Four Pages of The Sermon: A Guide to Biblical Preaching.* Nashville: Abingdon Press 1999.

Wiseman, Karyn L. *I Refuse to Preach a Boring Sermon: Engaging the 21st Century Listener.* Cleveland, OH: Pilgrim Press, 2013.

Notes

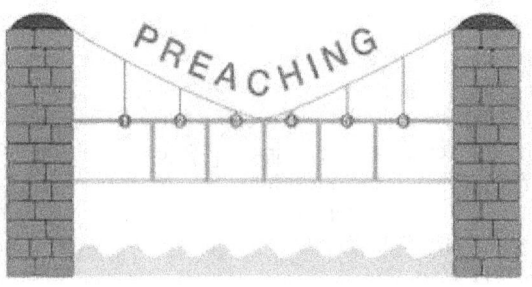

---

[1] John Fabarez, Preaching that Changes Lives (Eugene OR, Wipf & Stock, 2005), 4.
[2] Watson, Lance. That Was Then - This is Now: Properly Packaging Your Past. Richmond, VA. Forward Media and Publishing. 2013, LOC 1514.
[3] Watson, Lance. That Was Then - This is Now: Properly Packaging Your Past. Richmond, VA. Forward Media and Publishing. 2013, LOC 1539.
[4] Riddick, Dwight Sr. Does Preaching Have a Future? A Call to Join the Conversation. Bloomington, IN Universe 2015.

[5] Thomas. Frank. They Liked to Never Quit Praisin' God. The Role of Celebration in Preaching. Cleveland, OH. Pilgrim Press, 2013,

[6] Crowder, Stephanie. When Momma Speaks: The Bible and Motherhood from a Womanist Perspective. Louisville, KY. Westminister John Knox Press, 2016. XI,
[7] Crowder, Stephanie. When Momma Speaks: The Bible and Motherhood from a Womanist Perspective. Louisville, KY. Westminister John Knox Press, 2016. XI, 85
[8] Riddick, Dwight Sr. Does Preaching Have a Future? A Call to Join the Conversation. Bloomington, IN Universe 201573
[9] Eunjoo Mary Kim, Preaching in an Age of Globalization (Louisville: Westminister John Knox Press, 2010), 913, Kindle.
[10] Eunjoo Mary KimPreaching in an Age of Globalization, 922, Kindle.
[11] John S. McClure, Other-wise Preaching: A Postmodern Ethic for Homiletics (St Louis, MO: Chalice Press, 2001), 27
[12] Thomas, Frank. They Liked to Never Quit Praisin' God: The Role of Celebration in Preaching. Clevelena, OH. Pilgrim Press, 2013, Ebook LOC 248.
[13] David Augsburger, Pastoral Counseling across Cultures (Philadelphia: Westminster Press, 1986).
[14] Thomas, Frank. They Liked to Never Quit Praisin' God: The Role of Celebration in Preaching. Cleveland, OH. Pilgrim Press, 2013, 56.
[15] Laura Lundblad, Transforming the Stone: Preaching Through Resistance of Change (Nashville: Abingdon Press, 2001), 41
[16] Lundblad, Transforming the Stone, 43.
[17] Lundblad, Transforming the Stone, 43.
[18] Jana Childers, Performing The Word: Preaching As Theatre (Nashville: Abingdon Press, 1998), 30.
[19] Debra J. Mumford, The Reign of God: A Holistic Vision of Human Health (Louisville Article)
[20] Charles L. Bartow, God's Human Speech: A Practical Theology of Proclamation (Grand Rapids, MI: Eerdmans, 1997), 54.

[21] Otis Moss III, Blue Note Preaching in a Post-Soul World: Finding Hope in an Age of Despair (Louisville: Westminster John Knox, 2015), 7.
[22] Thomas, Frank. They Liked to Never Quit Praisin' God: The Role of Celebration in Preaching. Clevelena, OH. Pilgrim Press, 2013, Ebook LOC 248.
[23] Thomas, Frank. They Liked to Never Quit Praisin' God: The Role of Celebration in Preaching. Cleveland, OH. Pilgrim Press, 2013, 14.
[24] Debra Mumford, Exploring Prosperity Preaching: Biblical Health, Wealth, and Wisdom (Valley Forge, PA: Judson Press, 2012), 35.
[25] Henry Mitchell, Celebration and Experience in Preaching (Nashville: Abingdon Press, 2008), 133.
[26] Kristen Linklater, Freeing the Natural Voice (New York: Drama Book Publishers, 19760, 39.
[27] Jana Childers, Performing The Word: Preaching As Theatre (Nashville: Abingdon Press, 1998), 79.
[28] Childers, Performing The Word, 129.
[29] Bartow, God's Human Speech, 143.
[30] Jonah Sachs, Winning the Story Wars: Why Those Who Tell—and Live—the Best Stories Will Rule the Future (Cambridge, MA: Harvard Business Review Press, 2012), 210.
[31] Paul Wilson, The Four Pages of The Sermon: A Guide to Biblical Preaching (Nashville: Abingdon Press 1999), 166.
[32] Cleophas J. LaRue, I Believe I'll Testify: The Art of African American Preaching (Louisville: Westminster John Knox, 2011), 73.
[33] Leonard Sweet. "Giving Blood: A Fresh Paradigm For Preaching". Zondevan. Grand Rapids, MI. 198
[34] David Lose, Preaching at the Crossroads: How the World and our Preaching is Changing (Minneapolis: Fortress Press, 2013),
[35] Ian Stackhouse and Oliver D. Crisp, Text Message: The Centrality of Scripture in Preaching (Eugene, OR: Pickwick Publications, 2014), 38.